**W9-CNV-206**

**PLACE IN RETURN BOX** to remove this checkout from your record.
**TO AVOID FINES** return on or before date due.
**MAY BE RECALLED** with earlier due date if requested.

| DATE DUE | DATE DUE | DATE DUE |
|----------|----------|----------|
| FEB 13 2001 | | |
| OCT 23 2002 | | |
| | | |
| | | |
| | | |

1/98  c:/CIRC/DateDue.p65-p.14

# Conflict
# and Intervention
# in the Horn of Africa

## Bereket Habte Selassie

**Monthly Review Press**
**New York and London**

*Library of Congress Cataloging in Publication Data*

Bereket H. Selassie.
  Conflict and intervention in the Horn of Africa.
  Includes bibliographical references and index.
  1. Africa, Northeast—Politics and government—1974–
2. Africa, Northeast—Strategic aspects.
3. Ethiopia—Politics and government—1974–
4. Somalia—Politics and government—1960–
5. Somali-Ethiopian Conflict, 1977–1979.
6. National liberation movements—Ethiopia—Eritrea.
I. Title.
DT367.8.B47        960'.32        79-3868
ISBN  0-85345-534-1
ISBN  0-85345-539-2 (pbk.)

Monthly Review Press
62 West 14th Street, New York, N.Y. 10011
47 Red Lion Street, London WC1R 4PF

Manufactured in the United States of America

10 9 8 7 6 5 4 3 2 1

Hail the heroes of Sahel
Who feast on song and dance
After a hard day's fight
Carousing in the wilderness
With Kalashin and Bren
In the Sawra's solemn celebration.

Hail the Red Flowers and the Vanguards,
Being forged in the Fire of Sahel
To form the chain of the sentinel's vigil
To guard the front of the people's struggle
In their hands the Sawra is safe.
Fatuma! Abrehet! You're vindicated,
With all our submerged womanhood
Rejoice all! And embrace the revolution.

And sing to the glory of the martyrs
Who, in death, show us the way to life.
"And death shall have no dominion."
For they live in all our memories.

# Contents

## Maps

# Preface

This book is about conflict and intervention in an area lying within the region now known as the "arc of crisis," which includes the Horn of Africa, the Arabian peninsula, and the Gulf area beyond. The conflict in the Horn of Africa, more bloody than any since Vietnam, has recently been eclipsed by events in Iran and Afghanistan; but the issues are similar and geopolitically related, for the Horn and the Gulf are two sides of the same strategic coin, two aspects of the same struggle for dominion.

This study of the conflict in the Horn differs from the few that have appeared so far in that it reflects the perceptions and concerns of a man of the Horn, rather than the more external, strategically oriented interests of those who have written from the outside. It is at the same time a fresh attempt to study the entire region in its historical context.

The reader will find that in addition to the usual sources, I have drawn heavily on insights gained from personal knowledge of, and experience in, the area. I was born an Eritrean, but I have lived and worked in all parts of the Horn. My interest is more than academic, however. I feel the pain and suffering of a people caught in the tragedy and devastation of war.

I first thought of writing this book—or a version of it—when I was in the semi-liberated areas of the Eritrean highlands around Asmara in December 1974. I had escaped capture by the military junta—the Dergue—a few weeks earlier, and my friend and fellow Eritrean, General Aman Andom, the first leader of the

Dergue, had been killed for insisting on a negotiated settlement of the Eritrean war. That event was, I believe, a turning point in the recent history of Ethiopia and of the Horn, for reasons that I deal with in detail later in the book, but it also marked a turning point in my own life. The Dergue knew that as Aman's close friend and adviser, I had played a part in the development of his position on the Eritrean question; and I knew that they knew. I had to escape, or it would have been certain death, and I went to my native Eritrea, where I was warmly received as a "lost" brother come home. But writing the book had to wait, for in the meantime I became involved in the Eritrean people's struggle.

Many people have been helpful to me while I was writing this book. Special thanks are due to the following for reading drafts or parts of them and making helpful comments and suggestions: Claudia Carr, Tekie Fissehatsion, Sulaiman Nyang, Mulugeta Kebede, Peter Gabriel (Jibril) Robleh, Amaha Teferra, Lube (Zeude) Birru, Michael Moffit, and John Kakonge. My friend M.A.N., whose identity must remain hidden behind initials, has been a constant source of encouragement and stimulation, as well as a fount of useful current information on Ethiopia. I am grateful to him, and to all the other good people. Above all, I owe a special debt of gratitude to Susan Lowes of Monthly Review Press, for her patient and meticulous editorial work. Her comments (as the "average reader," as she called herself) and suggested changes have helped clarify a complicated story.

The writing of the book was made possible through a special grant from the academic vice-president of Howard University in the summer of 1978 and a fellowship grant from the Woodrow Wilson International Center for Scholars in the summer of 1979, for both of which I am deeply grateful. I would also like to note my deep appreciation for the support and kindness of my colleague Bob Cummings during the research and writing of the book.

# Conflict
# and Intervention
# in the Horn of Africa

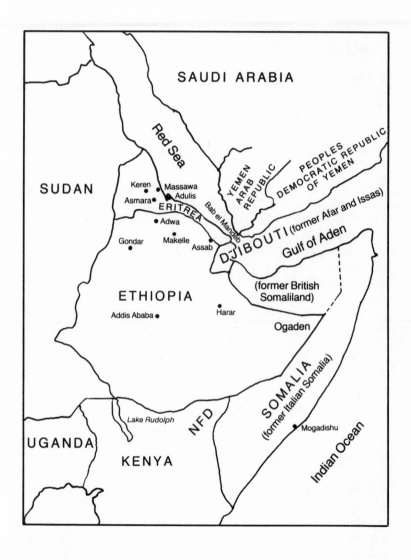

# Introduction:
# The Forces and the Issues

The Horn of Africa has been an arena of uninterrupted armed conflict for nearly two decades. This conflict, rooted in history and geography, has been aggravated by outside intervention for many years, most recently by the United States, in support of Haile Selassie, and by the Soviet Union, in support of Mengistu Haile Mariam's military regime, which was besieged and on the verge of collapse. This study is an attempt to define the elements of this conflict, and to present it in its historical context. In this introductory chapter, I will outline the contending forces and issues, the nature of the colonial and imperial legacies as they impinge on the region, the extent and nature of external military intervention, and the main national liberation movements both within Ethiopia and on its borders.


## The Roots of the Conflict

The Horn of Africa includes Ethiopia, Somalia, Djibouti, and Eritrea, and borders on the vital sea lanes of the Indian Ocean and the Red Sea, with the Arabian peninsula and Gulf region beyond.[1] At the southern end of the Red Sea lies the straight of Bab el Mandeb, while at the other end lies the Suez Canal. The opening of the canal in 1867 enhanced and internationalized the strategic and commercial value of the lands bordering the Red

1

Sea, and thus increased the possibilities of external intervention in the internal affairs of the region.

At the heart of the issues underlying today's conflicts in the Horn lie three legacies of the past: (1) The legacy of Ethiopian imperial expansion and conquest of people of different nations, speaking different languages, and having different economic livelihoods; (2) the legacy of European colonial rule, running parallel to, and at times cooperating with, Ethiopian imperial expansion; and (3) the legacy of outside imperialist intervention and economic penetration after World War II, with Ethiopia as the main focus.

## The Imperial and Colonial Legacy

The European colonial powers—Italy, Great Britain, and France—had installed themselves in the Horn of Africa by the end of the nineteenth century. In 1882 the Italian government took over the Red Sea port of Assab from the Rubattino Shipping Company, which had gained it through fraudulent purchase in 1869. The Italians then went on to occupy Massawa in 1885, and began to push into the highland interior of Eritrea. The French, who had a toehold in Djibouti, wanted to use this as a base to create a colonial territory in eastern Africa that would link with their west African possessions, but since this would have put a stop to the British dream of an empire from "Cape to Cairo," the British encouraged Italian ambitions in Eritrea. Every colonial power sent emissaries to the court of the Ethiopian emperor, Menelik, to intrigue against each other, and Menelik put this to good use. He concentrated on building a strong empire of his own by conquering territories to his south and by building a large army, using the spoils of conquest and his foreign contacts to purchase arms. Between 1887 and 1891, his army conquered Arusi, and in 1891 laid claim to an area slightly in excess of the present-day borders. By 1897 his right to all of Hararghe, the Ogaden, Bale, and Sidamo had been grudgingly recognized by the Europeans, while the British had established themselves in Somaliland. The border with Eritrea was recognized by Menelik in 1889 and confirmed in 1896. Ethiopia was a regional and imperial power in its own right.

After World War II, Great Britain and France gradually withdrew from direct control of their colonies—Somalia achieved political independence in 1960 and Djibouti in 1977—although their economies, like those of former colonies the world over, remained shaped by their economic ties to their former colonizers, and by their links to the wider capitalist market. On the other hand, the national groupings that had fallen to Menelik (whose mantle fell on Haile Selassie in 1916) never achieved even this much self-rule. The Tigray people, just south of Eritrea, the Oromo in the south and southwest, and the Somalis in the southeast all suffered the fate of conquered nations. And Eritrea, which shared the same right to independence enjoyed by almost every former European colony in Africa, was instead "federated" with Ethiopia in 1952, the result of a United Nations resolution that was sponsored by the United States, whose strategic interests in the area coincided with Haile Selassie's interest in Eritrea's human and material resources.

Colonial rule thus left behind it a patchwork quilt of states whose boundaries other African nations then swore to preserve. Every "colonial question," they declared, has a postcolonial solution, and not to agree to this was to be part of the problem. At issue are two conflicting principles, that of territorial integrity and that of the right to self-determination. The demand for territorial integrity, or national unity, is self-explanatory. Self-determination, on the other hand, although a historically valid and internationally accepted principle, is a kind of poor relation. It has been invoked by many an aggrieved minority struggling to assert its autonomy, identity, and cultural heritage. Yet invariably such an invocation has failed to draw a positive response from the international community—not necessarily for lack of good faith, but often because of the impossibility of resolving the two opposing claims. One principle is then endorsed at the expense of the other, which results in the denial of the basic human rights of minorities, which in turn may precipitate armed struggle. And so the problem persists, unresolved. The struggle in the Horn thus represents a historical challenge to colonially imposed solutions, and its implications reach far beyond the region.

But "stability"—as part of a general strategy of creating neo-colonial states that would be safe for foreign investment—was the cardinal principle of the postcolonial order. Its foremost theoretician was Harvard Professor Rupert Emerson, who argued that after independence "no residual right" to self-determination remained with any group that was within a postcolonial state or cut across its borders. Self-determination, he argued, was not a "continuing process," but only had the "function of bringing independence to people under colonial rule."[2]

This position was supported by the majority of African heads of state. Nkrumah was one exception. He advocated pan-African unity as a solution to this problem, rejecting colonial boundaries as arbitrary, unjust, and likely to lead to costly conflict. To that end he organized the All-African People's Conference in Accra from December 1958 to January 1959. He planned to lay the foundation for a unity, based not simply on government accords, but on people's political parties, labor unions, and so on. But the African people were organized at the national level by national interest groups, and there was as yet no unifying ideology with a continent-wide appeal; pan-Africanism was too weak and little known. Further, the African governments that had replaced the colonial rulers were ideologically divided—ranging from the Marxist government of Sékou Touré in Guinea to the semi-feudal regime of Haile Selassie in Ethiopia. The Organization of African Unity (OAU) therefore had to accommodate governments of different political persuasions.

The African nations decided upon their priorities at the second meeting of the OAU in Cairo in 1964, where a resolution was passed that recognized the colonially inherited borders, including those between Ethiopia and Somalia, as the basis for defining sovereign statehood. Even Nkrumah felt obliged to hold his peace. The only voices of dissent were Aden Abdullah, then president of Somalia, and the representative of Morocco, which had laid claim to Mauritania. The Somali government claimed that the resolution ignored the right to self-determination of those Somali who were not within the colonial borders, as well as their history of uninterrupted resistance to the British, the Ethiopians, and the Italians— and therefore implicitly that they were unique in the continent, so that the OAU rule should be proved by this exception.

Yet the Cairo resolution was as arbitrary as the colonial boundaries it sanctified. There was a bitter irony in this, since it came hardly a decade after decolonization had begun. Nonetheless, its arbitrariness was tolerable to the new African leaders in the absence of a readily available and universally acceptable alternative, and in the face of the current needs of the ruling groups.

An important aspect of the struggle in the Horn, then, is that it defies the Cairo resolution in at least two respects. First, the armed struggle in the Ogaden is a persistent reminder that the Cairo resolution did not do justice to all people.[3] Second, in failing, out of deference to Haile Selassie, to apply the same principle in Eritrea, the African leadership committed what may come to be regarded as their most glaring failure. Eritrea was an ex-colony like all the others, with colonial boundaries that defined its sovereign statehood. Yet Haile Selassie used his prestige and manipulative skills to keep the Eritrean question off the OAU agenda.

## Outside Intervention and Penetration

The failure of the African nations to address the national question, and the failure of international legal and moral principles to mediate between conflicting states, has made it possible for outsiders to intervene and impose their will. It has also invited a resort to arms and the development of a new form of dependency relationship between arms-supplying outside powers and their client states or nations. Thus, as we shall see in more detail later, the frustration of Somali national aspirations, and the denial to the Ogaden people of the right to self-determination, forced them to take up arms, and they went to whoever was willing to supply them, which at the time was the Soviet Union.

The fragility of the postcolonial African states, demonstrated by the army *coups d'état* that have changed three-quarters of their governments since 1965, has made it harder for their ruling groups to resist such a dependency. The politics of revolution, army style, has engulfed the Horn, with the military playing the dominant political role in Ethiopia, the Sudan, and Somalia. This has been in part due to the pressures of the "national" question, but at the same time social inequality, economic mismanagement and corruption, and a general lack of a just order of priorities have given rise to new lines of social division and struggle. In these conditions the armed forces, as the organized and armed segment of the urban petty bourgeoisie, have been able to play a critical role.

In the spring of 1974, two empires—the Ethiopian and the Portuguese—collapsed, loosening colonial and postcolonial bonds and prompting liberation fighters to redouble their efforts. The OAU was galvanized into helping the guerrilla fighters in Angola, Mozambique, and Guinea-Bissau, which by late 1975 had joined the family of independent states. Their hard-won independence sharpened African awareness of the relationship between ends and means, and introduced a new militancy into the OAU. Western diplomacy, which had confined itself to paying lip-service to the principle of self-determination, was forced to pay serious attention to the African voice.

In Ethiopia, the end of Haile Selassie's regime set the region afire, igniting liberation movements among oppressed nations or nationalities whose aspirations had been brutally suppressed. War in the Ogaden and Eritrea then threatened the new Ethiopian regime, and led the Soviet Union suddenly and dramatically to switch its allegiance from the Somalis to the Ethiopians, and to intervene militarily in both the Ogaden and Eritrea.

Today, as other African nations look on half-paralyzed and Soviet weapons destroy the lives of thousands, the struggle in the Horn continues. One of the great expectations of the Ethiopian revolutionary upsurge of the spring of 1974—that it would free the area from the historical burden imposed by the Ethiopian empire—has been denied. And indeed, as we shall see below, the formal abolition of feudal institutions, which was the great achievement of the revolution, did not and could not change feudal values, which survived to obstruct both the democratic revolution and the resolution of the national question.

As the Ethiopian military regime has, again with outside help, been able to reassert its control, it has continued to resort to military force and propaganda to deal with the national aspirations of the oppressed nations. The regime has adopted the rhetoric of Marxism and "proletarian internationalism," which has apparently convinced some Western nations—if not the inhabitants of the Horn—of its "radicalism," and has used, so far with success, the threat of a "foreign enemy" to win the allegiance of the Ethiopian people. It has fragmented the opposition, and increasingly resorted to a military solution as a way of resolving the national question—in Tigray, among the Oromo in the south, west, and southwest of the country, or in the Ogaden—and of avoiding a just resolution of the war in Eritrea. It has encouraged further outside intervention, in the form of military aid. But the inherited realities of the imperial past and the aspirations of the conquered nations cannot be so easily ignored. The desires of the people cannot be decreed away, and bloodily eradicating a critical opposition can only be a short-term solution.

# Part 1

## Empire, Nationalism, and Revolution

# 1

## Ethiopia:
## Foundations of an Empire-State

### The Twin Foundations

Ethiopia is an empire-state built in the nineteenth century, and inhabited by peoples of different nations (or nationalities) who speak over seventy languages and two hundred dialects. Its 1.22 million sq. km. cover contrasting geographical regions and climates, with high mountain ranges, deep gorges, forested areas, and flat grasslands, as well as arid and semi-arid deserts, and a great variety of flora and fauna.

The estimated population of about 27 million is composed of diverse nations and lives primarily in scattered rural villages, with agriculture, mostly in the highlands, and animal husbandry, mostly in the lowlands, being the livelihood of over 85 percent of the people and accounting for over 75 percent of national income. In a country endowed with good soil and other natural resources, the perennial phenomenon of famine has puzzled some observers, and Haile Selassie's "modernizing" rhetoric did not alter this. By a fatal irony of history, it was the drought of 1972–1973 (the famous "Wallo famine") that provoked the revolutionary explosion of February 1974 and ultimately led to the overthrow of the emperor's government.

Why did the "modernizing autocracy" not introduce reforms that would not only feed the people but would also increase the potential for development by providing the necessary surplus? Why did Haile Selassie in effect undercut his own economy?

11

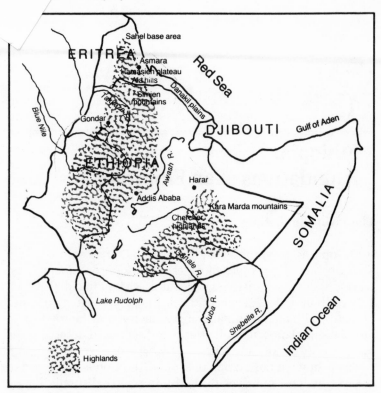

Highlands

Why did his government instead introduce changes in the institutions of government that had a "modern" guise but stop short of economic and social changes? The reasons for this failure lie in the feudal and imperial foundations of the Ethiopian state, which must be analyzed if Ethiopian politics, past and present, are to be understood.

## The Feudal Foundation

The structure of the Ethiopian state was based on a feudal system of land tenure. Over many centuries the northern and central highlands were slowly unified under a monarchy, with powerful feudal lords ruling semi-autonomous regions and paying tribute to the central kingdom. Control of land, the principal means of livelihood for the mass of the people, and its surplus produce was the central economic feature of the system. The use of the land and the disposal of its surplus produce were inextricably linked to the political system. First, the right to trib- ute from land—including arrangements such as *gult, maderia*, and so on—was granted for services rendered or to be rendered. The surplus produced from the land was sufficient to maintain a ruling class of royal family and courtiers, feudal lords and their retainers, high clergy and their hangers-on, and a vast peasant class that supported them. Second, the right to use the land— including *rist* and other types of land tenure arrangements—was held either because of membership in a lineage, or through suc- cessful litigation. In the latter case, the social status of the litigant was an important consideration in the judicial process. This feudal feature was one of the constant sources of conflict between the "modernizing" forces in Haile Selassie's regime, which sought to place law above personality, and the traditional forces, which resisted this, with the emperor mediating between the two.

The northern and central regions have been known as *yerist agher* (*rist* territory). Here the basic right of the peasant to a share in the land—*rist*—was inherited and derived from his member- ship in a kinship group. *Rist* rights are not forfeited even if a person is permanently absent from the land, a principle expressed by a legal maxim often heard in litigation:

> Yerist agher sew
> Beshi 'ametu—wederistu.[1]

(A man of a *rist* territory is entitled to his rights even after an absence of a thousand years.)

The ruling class appropriated the surplus produce from *rist* land principally through the mechanism of *gult*. Permanent *gult* rights were granted to the larger feudal lords and higher clergy, to churches and monasteries for the maintenance of their mem- bers, and to retired high officials as a reward for their services; *gult* was thus the principal compensation for officials until Haile Selassie introduced a salaried administrative class in 1931. Even after that, however, *gult* rights continued, and they persisted in some areas up until the eve of the revolution.

*Gult* rights were the result of a formal grant made by the monarch or a provincial feudal lord, and the conditions of the grant could vary. For instance, the *gultegna* (the grantee) might keep all of the revenue or might be required to send a portion of it to a higher feudal lord. He was also entitled to labor service from *ristegnas* (persons with *rist*) on his *gult* land, and since he was often a *ristegna* himself, he used this labor service for cultivation, weeding, and harvesting his own fields. He was exempt from tax on his own lands, and he collected special taxes in the course of carrying out administrative and judicial services on his *gult* land. All these functions gave him additional power and helped cement the entire feudal system. Feudal lords came to impose special taxes on "practically everything that lived or grew on the land, and on many forms of activity engaged in by the peasants."[2] In addition, the peasant rendered services and revenues to the church. And since Muslims were denied the right to own land, religious hegemony was co-terminous with class oppression.

The land and its produce thus became not only instruments of social control but a means to perpetuate oppression and poverty. The ruling class was well aware of the efficacy of *gult* and *rist* for keeping the peasants at the poverty level, as many Amharic proverbs illustrate, and used the Christian religious and local customary law to reinforce feudal relations.[3] Local law governed particular social relationships, but the *feteha negast*—the king's laws—were admininstered by the learned clergy and overrode local law. In addition to ties of religion, ties of kinship further cemented social life, making the demands of a *gultegna* acceptable.[4]

Commenting on these crosscutting social relationships, John Markakis and Nega Ayele have written:

> Strong vertical ties spanned the class divide. The divide itself was not a chasm. The aristocracy was multigraded, and its lowest ranks were barely discernible above the peasant masses among whom they lived. There were no marked cultural differences between the classes, nor any rigid social barriers. The aristocracy relied on ostentation, rather than cultivation or refinement, to maintain social distance.[5]

Indeed, the term aristocracy is hardly applicable to the Ethiopian feudal class, which did not patronize cultural or artistic activities until very late in Haile Selassie's regime, and even then these were poor imitations that impressed no one. Whatever artistic, literary, and cultural achievements the feudal class may have had to its name were actually the product of humble clergymen devoting their talents to the "glory of God." Destruction, rather than creativity, was the inherent characteristic of the feudal system.

The expansion of feudalism into southern Ethiopia—the *yeqign agher*, or conquered territory—produced a social structure and political situation that was markedly different from that in the north. These territories furnished the feudal Ethiopian state with its second basis, the imperial foundation.

## The Imperial Foundation

Unlike the northern and central region, where land is limited and the people have been forced onto increasingly smaller plots, the south is marked by an abundance of uncultivated land, which consequently has not played as significant a role as an instrument of social control. Before its conquest, the south contained a wide variety of socioeconomic modes, reflecting a variety of nationalities. None, however, had reached the degree of class division that characterized the north; on the contrary, most of the southern nations were characterized by a type of egalitarian communalism.

Menelik began the conquest of the southern region in earnest in the 1880s, and by the late 1890s Ethiopia included the rich agricultural provinces of Kaffa, Ilubabor, Wallaga, Sidamo, Gamu-Gofa, Arusi, Bale, and Hararghe (including the Ogaden). (Earlier, in the 1870s, Oromo-inhabited areas in Wallo had similarly had feudal relations superimposed upon them, but there the "conquest" had been a much slower process.) Immediately after the conquest he introduced the *sisso* system, whereby two-thirds of the land was confiscated and declared state property, while the remaining third was left to the "natives." The confiscated land was allotted to the major warlords, who had supported the conquest. These in turn subdivided their allotted territory according to feudal hierarchical principles, among their

officers, soldiers, and a vast body of retainers, according to rank. The smallest grant was at least one *gasha* (forty hectares), so that the greatest feudal lords overnight became owners of vast estates. In some cases, they owned whole provinces: Ras (prince) Birru, for instance, owned most of Arusi and parts of Chercher in Hararghe.

The bigger landowners soon became *gultegnas*, and then absentee landlords, leaving the administration of their estates to agents. Others subdivided their land among relatives, subordinates, and dependents. No feudal lord could claim to have properly settled his followers unless and until a church was built in the center of his new fiefdom, so churches and monasteries were constructed, and then they too received land grants, with labor and other services attached to them. Many learned clergy from the north thus began to move south, followed by a stream of settlers from the north and central regions, each of whom paid a small tax (or, initially, performed some state service), and received a land grant. The undistributed part of the confiscated land remained in the state's domain, and grants from it continued to be made until the revolution of 1974. Indeed, this was one of the most important ways in which Haile Selassie was able to buy off the emergent bourgeoisie. Feudalism was thus wedded to imperialism, producing the Ethiopian empire-state.

As for the unconfiscated third that was to be divided among the "natives," the lion's share was generally given away, along with *gult* rights, to local *balabats* (traditional leaders) for loyal service. The conquered nations thus found themselves suddenly enslaved, trapped in a system too omnipotent to resist and too omnipresent to escape. Their leaders were forcibly feudalized, their existence depending on the performance of services much like those performed by chiefs under British colonial rule in other parts of Africa.

The implications of this new feudo-imperial system were not immediately obvious, for the vast amounts of land and the need for labor service meant that tenants were rarely evicted in the days after the conquest. Nevertheless, they paid more tribute than they had ever paid before, ranging from one-third to one-half of their produce, as well as a 10 percent land tax (called *asrat*), which was more than a northern peasant paid. And more *corvée* labor was exacted from them than from those in the north. As Markakis and Nega put it: "Landlords, whether holding official positions or not, exercised administrative, police, and judicial functions within their estates, and used these powers to squeeze the last drop of surplus from the hapless workers of the soil."[6] Gradually some of the tenants were driven from the more fertile areas, while others were objects of raids for the slave trade.

Contrasting tribute in kind and labor service in the north and south, Markakis and Nega have written:

> In the case of the south, the imposition was greater in both forms because not only was a good deal more labor demanded, but the tribute imposed was considerably augmented to include what was essentially a payment of ground rent. The essence of this

payment was not clearly perceived at the time, since the peasant was left in control of his land, and the landlord remained beholden to the state in various ways by the condition of his grant. Consequently, the issue of possession remained hazy for several decades. When the haze was swept aside by economic and political currents in the period following the Second World War, it revealed the stark fact of irreparable loss of possession and the reduction of the southern peasant to tenancy.[7]

In addition, however, in the south the invaders introduced the privileges attached to the *gult* system without bothering to retain the safeguards inherent in *rist*, which were connected with kinship. The conquered southern peasant thus suffered a double jeopardy: he lost his right to land, and at the same time became subject to excessive tribute and exacting *corvée* labor.

Furthermore, the imperial component of the Ethiopian state was built on a trail of blood shed by innocent victims whose crime was to resist an alien invasion. Menelik's armies treated the conquered nations more harshly the more they resisted. Where resistance was total, the entire vanquished nation was sold into slavery, or declared subject to such sale, and its property confiscated. Thousands of able-bodied members of some national groups, such as the Kulo Konta and Wolaita, vanished as the conquering nation began to acquire a taste for owning and selling human chattel. It was indeed ironic that Mengistu, partly Kulo himself, should become the head of this imperial state.

The conquest included the imposition of an alien culture, religion (Christianity), and language. But the attempt to replace the national languages with Amharic was nowhere near as successful as the imposition of feudal legal values. The languages of the conquered nations persisted, as did the local cultures, and Ethiopia today, having abolished the feudal side of the state, remains saddled with this imperial heritage.

## The Feudal-Bourgeois Class and "Modernization"

Apart from superior military strength, Menelik's army benefited from the collaboration of some of the ruling groups of the conquered nations, particularly where kingdoms or chieftaincies already existed. The *balabats* worked hand in glove with the conquering ruling class, developing a new class alliance based on mutual economic interest. Some of the more important of them cemented these alliances with marriages. Yet as repositories of suppressed national sentiments and aspirations, the *balabats* remained close to their national compatriots, and generally received their support as well. When commercial agriculture was introduced in the 1950s, those who could balance this dual role often became thriving farmer-businessmen. Suppressed anger and hatred was directed more against the oppressor national group than the ruling-class alliance; not only had class consciousness not had sufficient time to develop and replace national consciousness, but the foreign feudal element was alien to the ways of the national ruling class.

As agriculture was increasingly commercialized and salaried administrative, security, and judicial personnel operating under a centralized administrative machine were introduced, the power of the feudal lords gradually weakened. The centralization process was begun by Menelik, but was more systematically pursued by Haile Selassie after 1930, and was hastened by the Italians during their occupation from 1936 to 1941. When the emperor returned from exile in 1941, he found that the Italians had left him with an impressive transport and communications system, which enabled him to launch his "modernization" drive. In 1931 he had moved against the more powerful feudal potentates, whom he still feared, by instituting a new constitutional and legal framework that undermined the economic basis of their independence. The new apparatus, however, was cumbersome and expensive, and did not spare the poor peasantry the burden of heavy taxation. Nor did it curtail the significant number of absentee landlords who claimed exorbitant dues from their tenants. Moreover, it encouraged members of the new bourgeoisie to become absentee landlords by granting them land, and drew important members of the feudal class into the world of commerce and agribusiness, either in joint ventures with the new bourgeoisie or with Western businessmen. The emperor was himself a shrewd businessman and owned a number of large estates.

The "modernizing" process also created a modest industrial sector, including textile and shoe manufacturing, and building construction. The guiding hand of Western, and especially United States, business interests became increasingly visible, and in the early 1960s laws were passed that made Ethiopia "safe for investment," particularly through tax holidays and profit repatriation rights. Gradually, and with the guidance of external business interests, a small but powerful commercial and bureaucratic bourgeoisie thus came into existence under the patronage of the emperor and his ministers. Those members of feudal families who had acquired the benefits of modern education saw their political power slipping away, but still had a semi-feudal economic base in the conservative countryside to back up their social position. Some tried to use that base to guarantee their existence as a class, and even to reassert their dominance; this led to an economic "marriage of convenience" between them and the upper echelons of the new bourgeoisie, centering around agribusiness and other land-related activities. The modern cash economy gained an added significance and impetus: money indeed became the "great solvent" of old values. The modest expansion of education resulted in the production of a few thousand educated "commoners" who used their new skills to acquire new interests and loyalties. They became the backbone of the bureaucratic bourgeoisie, and the feudal-bourgeois class alliance became a political fact. The emperor presided, manipulating the alliance to his advantage and using his secret security machine to watch it carefully.

"Modernization" also included the building of a modern defense system, the core of which was a large army organized around the principle of loyalty to the emperor and the monarchy. Here again the external (Western) connection is evident. From 1941 to 1950, the British were involved in training the Ethiopian army, and in 1953, with the signing of the U.S.–Ethiopia Defense Pact, the United States took over. The United States influenced military policy in Ethiopia until 1977 through its supply of military hardware, software, training, and advice. Building an educational system was a further part of this process, but here what the "modernization" did was to create the social forces—

teachers, students, organized industrial workers, and young army officers—that exploded in 1974.

In legal terms, the revised constitution of 1955 laid the foundation for the alliance between the new bourgeoisie and the feudal elements, while the civil and commercial codes of the early 1960s cemented it—providing proof, if proof be needed, that laws reflect the will and interest of a ruling class or alliance of classes. But the constitutional and legal framework must be set in the context of the drive provided by an energetic monarch, assisted by an educated class of ministers and technocrats. Thus laws were initiated by the emperor and his cabinet of "modern" men, who presented them to the legislative chambers (a lower house of elected deputies and a senate of appointed dignitaries) that had been created under the constitution. But while the initiative in the conception and design of the laws was in the hands of the bourgeoisie, the feudal elements were continuously on guard, protecting their vested interests, particularly when they were threatened by a new law. The emperor and his prime minister acted as arbitrators. The ways in which legislative duties were distributed between the two chambers served to bolster the bourgeoisie, but it also served the interests of the class alliance—an alliance that lasted until the revolution of 1974.

"One which is radical must be one which helps to reveal the truth."

# 2

## Ethiopia:
## Empire and Revolution

### Phase I: The Revolution and the "Creeping Coup"

Every system provides its own grave-diggers, as Marx once observed. The movement which exploded in Ethiopia in the spring of 1974 involved social forces unleashed by Haile Selassie's "modernization" process. The material basis for the alliance of the commercial/bureaucratic bourgeoisie and the thin upper crust of the "modernized" feudal class that dominated Ethiopian society on the eve of the revolution in 1974 was a cash-crop economy producing primarily coffee and oil-seed for export to foreign countries. The economy was thus linked to the capitalist market in a dependent relationship under which the development of agricultural self-reliance and industry were not priorities. As domestic food production fell and masses of unemployed moved into the urban centers, where they lived in subhuman conditions, there were sporadic protests and demonstrations, led by university students and teachers. The security apparatus, which took a lion's share of the government budget, was used to suppress such protests. In the absence of an organized and politically conscious mass movement, these uprisings remained isolated and were easily denounced by the ruling class as "divisive," "regionalist," or inspired by "foreign forces."

Protests began in earnest after the attempted coup of December 14, 1960, which was led by the head of the imperial bodyguard, who was in turn inspired by his radical civilian brother,

Germame Neway. Germame, a Columbia University graduate, had been involved in organizing a radical group and was suspected of "communist ties." He was thus sent as provincial governor to Jijiga in the Ogaden, but kept in touch with his brother and helped organize the coup during the emperor's absence. The "Decembrists" became martyrs in the eyes of politically conscious Ethiopians, and their martyrdom provided the impetus for agitation that lasted over the next decade. Event followed event, and by the spring of 1974 the "creeping coup" had become a reality.

Several forces and events were of key importance in encouraging this process. First, the rise in the world price of oil and the government's decision to increase gasoline prices by 50 percent led to a strike by taxi drivers that crippled the capital city. Thousands of their passengers were sympathizers. This was followed by the first general strike in Ethiopian history, held between March 7 and 11, 1974, and led by the labor unions that were the product of Haile Selassie's industrialization program. Their strike, and their demands, were a crucial factor in the developing revolution.

Second, a World Bank-inspired review of the educational sector was interpreted by the teachers as a threat to their class interests,[1] and they too went on strike. The 17,500 teachers constituted more than half of the professional class and were thus the core of the petty bourgeoisie.[2] Not only were they effectively organized, but their services were vital and they had links with the university and high school students, who had been actively agitating for change for a decade. Both teachers and students were another product of the "modernization" process, this time the modernization of education.

Third, a crushing defeat in Eritrea in December 1973 and January 1974 precipitated an army mutiny, unheard of in the history of the Ethiopian army, that eventually exploded into a full-scale revolt. Young officers, a further product of the modernization campaign, were waiting for an opportune moment to seize power for themselves. Then, in mid-January 1974, a unit in Negelle in Sidamo province, led by junior officers, NCO's, and enlisted men, mutinied and detained their commanding officer in a protest against their living conditions. The chief of ground forces was dispatched by the emperor to "solve the problem," but he was taken prisoner and forced to eat the same food and drink the same muddy water that was at the root of the complaints. When he could not take it any more he was sent back to the capital, a physical and nervous wreck.

By then the "Negelle flu" had spread. Army units in Asmara imprisoned their officers and then presented a list of grievances, labor-union-fashion, and demanded immediate redress. One item on the list referred to the lack of concern on the part of the government in general, and the high command in particular, for the fate of the many soldiers fighting in Eritrea. It noted that the families of high-level officers were sent abroad for medical treatment of minor ailments, while their comrades-in-arms were left for hyenas to feast upon, and nobody took care of their families. This was an emotionally charged issue that touched a cord throughout the army and neatly divided it across class lines. The Asmara mutiny was pivotal in pushing forward the course of the revolution. It added momentum to the revolt started at Negelle, and gave courage to army units in other parts of Ethiopia. It struck terror into the hearts of the ruling class, which then, as now, linked its fate with an Ethiopian victory in the Eritrean war. And the Dergue was able to use the Asmara demands to rally support for itself.

The fourth, and precipitating, factor was the disastrous drought and subsequent famine in Wallo and Tigray provinces in 1972 and 1973 which claimed the lives of over 200,000 people and provided a common ground around which the various forces could rally. The emperor's government not only failed to provide any disaster relief for the victims, but kept this a secret so that no national or international relief could reach them. A BBC-TV producer, Jonathan Dimbleby, uncovered the disaster and his reports shocked the world.[3] His camera caught the haunting faces of starvation and death, alongside the opulent life led by the imperial court and its entourage, unconcerned in the face of mass starvation. When news of the disaster reached Ethiopia, students organized fasts and donated the modest proceeds of their sacrifice to the survivors of the famine. Others donated money and their time. Haile Selassie's government was seen to be not only corrupt, but totally unable to organize any relief efforts in time to save lives. The famine, like the other factors that led to the coup, was also a result of the "modernization" campaign. For the roots of "natural" disasters lie in the social relations of production—in particular, the loss of control over the means of production (land) and hence over production and food resources. And this was directly related to the effects of the feudal system of land use.

The stage was thus set for the snowballing army revolt and the popular upsurge of the spring of 1974. When the mutinies started in late February, the prime minister, Aklilu Habte Wold, resigned, along with his entire cabinet. This left the 83-year-old emperor a captive of the feudal elements around his court, headed by his kinsman Ras Asrate Kassa, who saw a chance to reinstate himself and his class. He counseled that nothing short of class solidarity could save the situation, and that a close kinsman (i.e., himself) should take charge of the government. The emperor did not trust Asrate, and instead chose British-educated Endalkachew Mekonnen, a one-time candidate for the post of UN secretary-general and a personification of the "modernized" aristocracy. Endalkachew faced four immediate tasks: (1) he had to choose a cabinet; (2) he had to come to terms with all the social forces unleashed by the revolution—labor unions, army, students and teachers, and so on; (3) he had to keep "law and order"; and (4) he had to put together a government reform program that would buy him some time.

### The Origins of the Dergue

Endalkachew was faced with a growing opposition from sections of the military, which coalesced in the formation of the Dergue, the body that was able, by an intricate series of steps that successively destroyed the supports of the old ruling class, to overthrow the emperor and establish itself firmly in control. This completed the first phase of the revolution.

The Dergue—the word means "committee" in Amharic—had its origins in a group of officers in the Addis Ababa garrisons, who were isolated, unknown, and inexperienced, but were united in their demands for better pay and living conditions for themselves and their families. As the events of February unfolded, however, they became haunted by the specter of a dictator emerging as the new leader—motivated as much by genuine nationalist feeling as by the threat to their class interest as an elite officer corps that such an event would constitute. On June 28, 1974, each unit of the armed forces sent a representative to a meeting where a coordinating committee of the armed forces, police, and territorial army was established. This was what came to be known as the Dergue. Its members had begun as primary and junior secondary level officers. They were similar to the common soldier, and thus could feel sympathetic to their frustrations, yet they had had a more modern education, were ambitious, and had been promoted through the ranks. The result was that they did not address themselves to the burning issues that affected the bulk of the people, and had no political program that would rally them. They depended on the students, teachers, and labor unions for support, but were also threatened by each of these. They vacillated, and finally called upon General Aman Andom to lead them. As early as February, Aman had been in touch with the military committee which was coordinating events in Addis, at times meeting with the group daily and working out strategies for the conduct of the revolution. Aman had a clear insight into the psychology of the oppressor/exploiter class, an insight he had gained during ten years of "banishment" in the Ethiopian senate. His working principle was to place the property of the ruling class in jeopardy, forcing them to submit in the hope that they would be able to hit back after they regained their freedom. The media was skillfully used to translate this strategy into action: for instance, all dignitaries were asked to give themselves up or have their property confiscated. They fell into the trap, filing in one by one—with the notable exception of Tsehayu Inkua-Selassie and his brothers. If at this point, before the military had consolidated its power, the opposition had taken a firm line, the conservative countryside might have been won over to their side. This would have been fatal to the as yet unorganized military junta, which still, as a matter of tactics, professed loyalty to the emperor. The emperor, considerably shaken, seemed to side with the forces of change, urging recalcitrant members of the old government to submit. Tsehayu, who knew the emperor well, did not respond to the call for collaboration. He rebelled instead. It took several months and a minor battle before he was defeated.

In the early stages, Atnafu Abate, who was coordinator of the armed forces under the guidance of Aman, was chairman of the Dergue. But among those who attended the organizational meeting was Mengistu, elected as a representative of his unit in Jijiga. Personal rivalries and national animosities arose within the Dergue immediately and threatened its dissolution. In a crucial meeting, the members decided that Atnafu, who was from the ruling Amhara nation, had to be replaced by a "neutral." Mengistu appeared perfect: he was reportedly an Oromo, and the son of a former slave.[4]

At the time the Dergue was being formed, the military was being criticized by left groups. The demands it was making were mostly for improving their own working conditions and standard of living, and crowds sang songs that called them sectarian, selfish, and cowardly for limiting their demands to economic issues. University students, supported in particular by young airforce and army aviation officers, showered Addis Ababa with an endless stream of leaflets urging the military to turn their claims to political demands. These pamphlets were avidly sought and read by the public, and had a crucial influence on subsequent events. The military demands took an increasingly radical turn, including a demand for a commission of inquiry, and the slogan "land to the tiller"—an old favorite of student radicals. On the whole, however, the military did not as yet present a well-thought-out strategy for social and political change.

Throughout this first period, neither the emperor nor Endalkachew could rely on any one class for support. The new bourgeoisie, which Endalkachew sought to lead, lost its nerve in the face of growing unrest on the part of the trade unions and students, and of the increasingly intransigent behavior of the armed forces. The Dergue's growing confidence was manifested in arrogant demands and sudden reversals of cabinet plans. The dominant group within it came from a petty-bourgeois class of small tradesmen and low-ranking government employees, and their mood reflected their accumulated hostility to the conspicuous consumption of the feudal-bourgeois state in the face of widespread poverty, ignorance, and disease. The cabinet, intimidated, failed to give Endalkachew the backing he needed to galvanize a confused bourgeoisie into opposing military rule. Nothing worked for him. His class background and personality, as well as the insoluble conflict of interests, made it impossible for him to unite the country. There were mass demonstrations calling for his resignation and detention—to join other former ministers, who had been arrested by the armed forces. When he too was taken prisoner—at his own cabinet meeting—it was clear that the role of the cabinet, and of the bourgeoisie it represented, was fast diminishing.

The Dergue was systematically gaining control of critical levers of power. This was to be no classic *coup d'état*, but a slow-motion coup, which struck at the bases of power one by one. The complexity of the system and the division of the army along class, ethnic, and factional lines necessitated patience. The Dergue thus appointed another civilian prime minister, an aristocrat known for his Fabian socialist views. At the same time, however, it dealt quickly with the constitutional commission that had been established on popular demand and had worked for five months to draft a new constitution (of bourgeois-democratic vintage): the constitution was simply shelved and the old parliament unceremoniously dismissed. Aman then proposed the formal deposition of the emperor, and although this was at first resisted by several influential members of the Dergue, including Mengistu, on "tactical" grounds, Aman finally persuaded them that the emperor was not only an anomaly in a revolution, but was a source of danger because counter-revolutionary forces could rally around him. The motion was carried, and the formal deposition was proclaimed on September 12, 1974. This date may be regarded as the high point of the revolution and it is the date celebrated as Revolution Day. When the emperor was taken from his palace in a small Volkswagon, masses of people thronged the streets of Addis Ababa thundering, "Robber! Robber!" It was the end of Haile Selassie, and the end of an era.

The Dergue then issued a proclamation (see Appendix 2) formally replacing the emperor as head of state. Prior to this, few had known its membership, which was now revealed to be 120 men, officers below the rank of major and enlisted men, representing all units of the armed forces, police, and the old militia, known as the territorial army.

The reasons for the Dergue's anonimity were several. First, it was necessary to protect its members, at a time when the old regime was far from finished. Second, the armed forces, which had been deliberately divided by the emperor, had to be brought together and this necessitated coordination and secrecy in order to avoid betrayals and jealousies based on unit rivalries. And third, the Dergue was responding to an Ethiopian penchant for intrigue, and fostered the atmosphere of secrecy, which fascinated the nation. It never officially revealed its size and composition, and, with the exception of the top few positions, its members' names remained secret.

The highest ranking members were a few captains, including Mengistu and Atnafu (first and second vice-chairmen after Aman became chairman in August 1974). A few of the officers were graduates of the prestigious Harar military academy, but most had attended the one-year Holeta military school. The majority of the NCO's and enlisted men had not attended such schools; many lacked a secondary education. The manner of their selection for membership in the Dergue was equally varied. While many were appointed by their commanding officers, some—like Mengistu—were chosen by their units because they were known troublemakers who were dispatched to the center of the storm. No one imagined that the storm would produce such a mighty flood. Later, when the importance of the Dergue's role was realized, several units wanted to replace their earlier choices but found it was too late: the members found the exercise of the combined powers of emperor and prime minister too exciting.

While anonimity sheltered the Dergue from outside pressures, its size and diverse composition rendered it ineffective, particularly in a fast-moving situation. After June 28, 1974, various committees were established, and their chairmen made all decisions in the name of the whole organization, soon becoming a de facto executive council.

The removal of the emperor brought Aman to the pinnacle of state power; it also exposed him to the perils of a power struggle. On November 7, 1974, a confrontation took place between him and the dominant group, led by Mengistu, over the war in Eritrea. Aman, an "Ethiopianized" Eritrean, proposed a peaceful solution that met with virulent opposition and suggestions that he was motivated by a desire to help the Eritreans.[5] He resigned in opposition to a "military solution," and died two weeks later when he resisted the Dergue's attempt to have him arrested.[6] Immediately thereafter, the Dergue, meeting in a frenzied night session, decided to execute fifty-nine people, including a few of the radical officers who had supported Aman's motion. The motive was apparently a desire both to cover up the true reason for Aman's death and to dilute its effects with the news of the mass execution of corrupt officials.

Aman's death—and the fact that he was Eritrean by origin and that he had laid down his life rather than send an expedition into Eritrea—had an unexpected effect. Within a few weeks, thousands of Eritreans left Ethiopia to go over to the Eritrean side, to be joined by thousands more when the Ethiopian military escalated the war in February 1975, bombing and burning villages and massacring defenseless people. Ironically, and as Aman himself predicted in his last days, his death served the Eritrean cause.

## Phase II: The Dergue and the Left

The period between the formal overthrow of the emperor in September 1974 and the summer of 1975 saw the reversal of the creeping coup. A series of events occurred in quick succession, producing a momentum of their own and leading the Dergue to take desperate and contradictory steps. The crisis of November

1974 that led to Aman's death was the first such event, pre-cipitating as it did the escalation of the war in Eritrea, beginning on February 1, 1975. It marked a turning point in the recent history of the Horn, as we shall see later.

The second event was the National Campaign for Develop-ment Through Cooperation, or ZEMECHA, which was launched in December 1974 to explain the revolution to the peasant masses. All university and senior high school students were to go into the countryside for a period of two academic years. Most of these students, however, were leftist supporters of the Ethiopian People's Revolutionary Party (EPRP), and with the party's gui-dance agitated against the ZEMECHA on the ground that it was designed to remove the left opposition from the cities—a charge that was only partially true, since many in the Dergue sincerely believed in the ZEMECHA. In the end, the students were forced to go, but they decided to use the ZEMECHA to educate and organize the peasants in support of political demands, includ-ing the demand for people's government, all contrary to the Dergue's intentions. The absence from Addis and other main urban centers of university and senior high school students enabled the Dergue to concentrate its efforts on neutralizing and eventually destroying the conservative forces. In this it had the valuable services of those leftist groups willing to help.

The ZEMECHA campaign raised the democratic conscious-ness of the peasant masses to a degree unforeseen by the military. The students and teachers conducted the campign with vigor, consciously adhering to democratic principles. For the most part, they were careful not to command but to guide and advise, encouraging the peasants to follow open and democratic proce-dures, thus breaking the age-old tendency to secrecy and the habit of obeying the commands of superiors. As Markakis and Nega have observed:

> After they overcame the peasants' initial mistrust, the campaigners threw themselves into the task of association organization. Once these were formed, they were guided toward self-assertion vis-à-vis the central government and its local representatives. They were also urged to take militant action toward their former op-pressors. The students fostered the class consciousness of the

poor peasant, and encouraged him to segregate his enemies and to exclude them from the associations.[7]

The campaigners also encouraged the peasants to give the associations' judicial committees jurisdiction over all civil and criminal matters, which undermined the power of the police and judges, who represented the central state. In short, the campaigners "sought to foster a large degree of peasant self-government in order to prevent the bureaucratization of the new economic and social order which would subject the peasantry to the rule of what was derogatorily described as 'petty-bourgeois socialism.' " The Dergue initially cooperated with the campaigners by sending experts and administrators to coordinate their efforts, and a cadre of petty bourgeoisie was formed in the countryside that represented both a "hope for ushering in a new era and a threat that this hope might be snared and stifled in a net woven by the new bureaucracy." In the cities, the labor unions were infiltrated by EPRP cadres, and, operating through the Confederation of Ethiopian Labor Unions (CELU), they too demanded that a provisional people's government be established.

The third event was the anti-feudal reform that abolished the tenancy system, and the nationalization of several enterprises and of urban land. These reforms were a serious attack on the socioeconomic base of the feudal class, and were in response to the popular demand for land reform; they were thus an attempt to "legitimize" the new regime's power. But there was no political organization that could organize, defend, and carry forward the revolution in the name of the masses—the supposed beneficiaries—and the Dergue was thus reluctantly forced to allow members of MEISON (the Amharic abbreviation for the All-Ethiopian Socialist Movement, a coalition of several groups) to work out a strategy of political education and organization of the masses.

The civilian left in Ethiopia, at first excluded from power by the Dergue, had responded in different ways. On the one hand, the EPRP had demanded that power be immediately handed over to a provisional people's government. It argued that the Dergue represented the petty bourgeoisie and thus could not be trusted to lead the revolution in the name of the great mass of peasants and workers. On the other hand, MEISON at first offered "critical support," their differences with the Dergue being basically matters of tactics. MEISON maintained that the military was the only organized and armed group capable of defending the achievements of the revolution, and that the EPRP's demand for a provisional people's government would have a counter-revolutionary effect because it would introduce into the government elements whose loyalties to the masses were questionable. The EPRP, however, rejected this on the grounds that the military, as represented by the Dergue, would use its power for the interests of its own class. The Dergue itself had an ambivalent relationship to the left groups, needing their support and thus courting them, but also fearing and distrusting them. Some more radical elements in the Dergue advocated a dialogue, or even a sharing of power, but as the EPRP and MEISON diverged in the policies they advocated, the Dergue followed the oppressor's instinct to divide and rule, and allowed a working arrangement with MEISON only.

The EPRP then began to attack MEISON for joining forces with the Dergue, which it now began to call a "military dictatorship." The battle of the pamphlets was on, and continued from the fall of 1975 into the spring of 1976. The debate centered on the control of state power and the role of the masses, occasionally turning to the Eritrean question. To the EPRP's repeated demand that power be handed over to a provisional people's government, MEISON reiterated that the Dergue was the only organized and armed group that could defend the revolution until the masses were politically, educationally, and organizationally armed. On the Eritrean question, the EPRP supported self-determination in principle, while MEISON at first dodged the issue.

The Dergue watched this debate with intense interest, subtly hinting to MEISON that its line was correct, and that it would hand over power soon. Yet what in fact happened was that the Dergue did not show any signs of doing so—on the contrary, it consolidated its power at the expense of all other social forces—while MEISON became increasingly isolated from the masses.

MEISON had never had deep roots in the mass movements of the city or the countryside, primarily because its leadership was made up of foreign-educated intellectuals, while the EPRP's base was in the national university in Addis Ababa and the high schools, both of which had had ties with the labor movement since the early 1960s.

One result of the MEISON/Dergue alignment was a curious process of one up-manship, in which the Dergue/MEISON axis tried to "out-left" the EPRP in the battle for the loyalty of the Ethiopian masses—a battle that was to have far-reaching consequences.

The ZEMECHA produced some unexpected results. In Kaffa province, where the families of some of the deposed landlords resisted and the students became engaged in pitched battles with them, the police sided with the landlords. When the students protested to the Dergue, it backed the police in the name of "law and order." The EPRP, through its newspaper, *Democracia*, then attacked the Dergue and MEISON as anti-revolutionary, and their newly proclaimed "Ethiopian socialism" as unscientific and utopian.

The EPRP's militant stand and theoretical "sophistication" were not, however, matched by a strong organization or a sufficient number of disciplined cadres who could organize and lead the masses. Put on the defensive on ideological grounds, and threatened with mass resistance, the Dergue placed increasing reliance on the state apparatus, including the media and the forces of violence. The Dergue's determination to hold onto power at any cost was increasingly shared by MEISON, which quickly became a willing tool in the service of the Dergue, whatever its slogans and programs. It took part in dismantling the peasant associations that the ZEMECHA and land reform measures had created by infiltrating them with its members and by drafting the peasants to fight in Eritrea and the Ogaden.

In the cities, confrontation had begun to take a violent form as early as September 1975, when the EPRP organized a protest march to celebrate the anniversary of the emperor's overthrow. Students and workers participated, the students having traveled from the ZEMECHA areas and the workers taking part after a clandestine CELU congress. The Dergue confronted the march with armed power, and there were many deaths and injuries.

The CELU then demanded democratic rights, and threatened a general strike.

On September 25, the Dergue decided to teach the opposition a lesson. The military invaded a CELU meeting, shot seven workers, and wounded several others. The CELU, however, did not have the organizational strength or tactical ability to mount a protest in the face of a determined, or entrenched, military group, and the several spontaneous strikes that followed could not be sustained.

MEISON now thought it saw a chance to use the Dergue to its advantage. It offered a slogan—"Educate the masses, organize them, and arm them!"—and proposed a provisional political bureau to be in charge of organizing the people. It selected fifteen people, the majority of whom were leading MEISON cadre, to be its members, and launched its campaign. The EPRP was of course excluded. MEISON members were also appointed to ministerial and to other executive positions, which accelerated the reform campaigns. MEISON also saw the CELU as a threat, and persuaded the Dergue to replace it with a new labor union, and to promulgate new industrial relations legislation. All these measures were designed to recruit a nuclei of leadership for mass organizations who were loyal to MEISON.

This set the stage for the final split within the left. The EPRP was no match for MEISON in this early, polemical, stage of the battle, for the simple reason that MEISON had access to all the resources of the state, including the media. Partly in order to give the illusion of abiding by democratic rights and "fair play," but mainly in order to identify those who supported the EPRP, the Dergue agreed to a "democratic dialogue" in the spring of 1976, to discuss the future of all levels of social and economic life. Discussion groups were formed within all the state-owned enterprises, in government departments, and in other areas. But it soon became clear that proclamation and practice were not the same thing. Workers' discussion groups were watched, and active leadership identified and picked up at opportune moments.

On April 20, 1976, the National Democratic Revolutionary Program (NDRP) was proclaimed. It was to lead Ethiopia toward the establishment of a people's republic, and was accompanied by a nine-point program that would lead the way toward the achievement of autonomy—and would solve the Eritrean question. All of these measures were proclaimed and discussed extensively by the media.

These events were accompanied by the widespread use of the media to discredit the EPRP as "anarchist" and the Eritrean struggle as a "tool of Arab power politics." The EPRP itself declared war on the Dergue/MEISON axis by declaring all the members of the politbureau, the council of ministers (including its chairman, Mengistu), and the Dergue itself, as well as some of its vocal bureaucratic supporters, enemies of the revolution who had to be eliminated. This was no empty threat: the EPRP had decided to wage an urban guerrilla war rather than a protracted rural-based people's war, and had carried out several assassinations in broad daylight.

The media did not attack only the EPRP. During the spring of 1976, a series of campaigns were launched against "economic saboteurs," who were accused of causing the shortages of food and other basic items that had led to soaring prices. The real cause of the shortages was a combination of unrealistic, hastily designed government measures and hoarding. The Dergue- and MEISON-dominated politbureau thus blamed their own failure on traders and bureaucrats, who became the victims of a new type of terror. The politbureau recruited members from the mass of unemployed urban youth—the lumpenproletariat—to carry out these arrests. Large numbers were armed and patrolled the streets of Addis Ababa in late 1976 and early 1977. People began to see them as MEISON cadres who had been given permission to kill anyone suspected of being against the regime.

It was not until July 1976 that certain elements within the Dergue began to see the light—the democratic light. Mengistu's growing autocratic power had practically reduced the Dergue to a rubber stamp, and his blind spot on the Eritrean question, and on the national question within Ethiopia, had bled the country, literally as well as figuratively, financially, and economically. In early 1976 a faction of the Dergue, led by Captain Sisay Habte, pushed for a "peace plan" on Eritrea. This was interesting because Sisay had never before favored a peaceful dialogue with the guerrillas—and in fact, when General Aman had proposed a peaceful solution in November 1974, it was Sisay who had accused him of disloyalty and of favoring his "Eritrean brothers." But Sisay's differences with Mengistu were really only of a tactical nature: he recommended a "symbolic withdrawal" of some Ethiopian troops from Eritrea, as a "sign of good will." Since he was as responsible as Mengistu for the costs of the Eritrean war, he could not have survived a true peace, and his "peace initiative" must be seen as a tactic in a struggle for personal survival, as the groundwork for an anti-Mengistu *coup d'état*.

Sisay went to Eritrea, accompanied by Haile Fida, a MEISON leader. In Asmara, he wrote a letter to the Eritrean People's Liberation Front (EPLF) and sent them a hand-picked group of Eritrean elders with peace "feelers." But the terms of the letter were vague and evaded the main issues, and it was rejected. Sisay then persuaded General Getachew Nadew, military governor of Eritrea and commander of the Ethiopian armed forces there, to support his coup.[8] His plan was apparently to have units of the Ethiopian army stationed in Asmara draw up a list of demands and present them to Mengistu, which would lead to a more general uprising—all an echo of 1974, although this time the chosen slogan was "Dialogue, not war." This was a worthy objective, one that in addition had great appeal to the war-weary armed forces in Eritrea. Indeed, Mengistu's fall, when it comes, will originate in Eritrea, as he well knows. But in July 1976, after returning to Ethiopia, Sisay was surprised by Mengistu, and he, Getachew, and a few others were executed.

Some members of the Dergue began to be alarmed at Mengistu's penchant for summary executions of his political rivals. They did not plan so drastic a step as a coup, however. A faction, led by Alemayehu Haile, chairman of the administrative committee, and Captain Mogues Wolde-Mikael, chairman of the economic committee, decided instead to call for "democratic dialogue" and for a united front of all progressive democratic forces in the country, including the EPRP. In June 1976, the Alemayehu group anonymously published a pamphlet entitled "The Unity and Difference of Clandestine Parties and Movements on the Question of a National Front." It was criticized by the Dergue, probably at MEISON's instigation, for daring to favor a democratic dialogue with the EPRP. MEISON was fearful of the EPRP's greater following, and perhaps of eventual vendettas. As *Addis Fana*, the semi-official monthly, put it later (in the April 1977 issue):

> The principal aim of the pamphlet was to present the EPRP as progressive and revolutionary, and to cause the Dergue to accept it [the EPRP] as progressive on the grounds that it had a strong popular basis and a large following, so that it becomes necessary to cooperate and create unity with it.

The pamphlet soberly analyzed the alignment of progressive forces in the country, their relationships and differences. It listed the issues on which the various parties or movements agreed or disagreed, including the national front with the Dergue, the Eritrean question, the national liberation struggles among the Tigreans, Oromo, and Afar, and the role of mass organizations, including labor unions, students, teachers, and peasants. After analyzing the respective positions of the EPRP and MEISON on all these questions, the pamphlet concluded that the EPRP's position was the more acceptable. It also agreed with the EPRP on the issue of democratic participation of the masses, and on the question of forming a national front of all progressive forces.

Explaining its conclusion on the national front, the pamphlet stated that all Ethiopian revolutionary groups were anti-feudal, anti-imperialist, and anti-bourgeois, and that the main question therefore was how to unify these groups against their common enemies. This comment was followed by a passage that surely did not endear its writers either to MEISON or to Mengistu. It read:

> In order to create the favorable conditions which would enable them to create a united front for the struggle, *the democratic right of the oppressed masses must be guaranteed as a precondition.* (Emphasis in original.)

This was followed by a discussion of the necessity of a united front that is worth quoting at length, because it became the focus of the attack by MEISON and Mengistu:

*The necessity of a front.*

(1) On the stage of national democratic revolution, different classes struggle together for a common interest. Therefore the proletarian party needs to harness progressive forces which will struggle with it, and (2) at the same time the proletarian party, at the stage when it cannot emerge victorious alone and gain state power (this can only happen in a socialist revolution), has to unite with such forces to fight against the common enemies and (thus) guarantee future success.

Then comes a broadside clearly aimed at MEISON:

If by any chance, it is said that, in order to guarantee democratic rights and to create a united front, it is necessary to educate and organize the masses, this constitutes a denial of the fact that a guarantee of democratic rights itself creates the most favorable condition for such an education, organization, or struggle. It is tantamount to saying: "Let me educate you," having first withheld the weapon for doing so. It amounts to arrogating to oneself what belongs to the masses, and it is self-defeating in the final analysis.

It can be seen that here was an unqualified belief that once unlimited democratic rights were given to the masses, they would know their common interests and their differences and could be trusted to compose those differences in order to protect their common interests. As for the MEISON/Mengistu policy, the pamphlet stated:

At the present time, as things stand, the delay of the guarantee of democratic rights only serves to aggravate the differences among the different progressive forces who would turn against each other instead of joining forces against the common enemies. Secretive moves and conspiracies would be exposed to public view, which would make it easier to judge who is progressive and who is reactionary.

The pamphlet concluded with a reasoned appeal for a united front. In essence, it said that the establishment of a national front was not only a necessity but a duty on the part of all progressive parties and movements in the new national democratic stage. Only through a united front could existing contradictions be resolved by peaceful means, i.e., in a democratic dialogue. If the various groups could not resolve their contradictions through peaceful means, this meant there must be a contradiction between them and the masses. Any party or movement that is in contradiction with the masses could not organize or lead them. Therefore, all parties or movements that are truly anti-feudal, anti-bureaucratic-capitalist, anti-imperialist, and against all supporters of these, must form a united front and fully participate in the revolution.

The pamphlet's general praise for the EPRP did not mean it was completely uncritical: "No party or group should aim or attempt to liquidate another," it said. "Instead, there must be an attempt to resolve any contradictions through peaceful means . . . but some of the anti-revolutionary steps taken by the party must be stopped. The EPRP has to abandon such anarchist tendencies, for otherwise it may forfeit its rightful place as a revolutionary organization."

Three months after the publication of the pamphlet, the Alemayehu group took a further step in its democratic route. In September 1976, it successfully organized a mini-coup within the Dergue, which limited Mengistu's power to the chairmanship of the council of ministers, and made General Teferi Banti, the avuncular officer who had succeeded Aman, the titular head of the Dergue. Unfortunately, however, the members of the revolutionary-democratic faction suffered from the virtues of the cause they espoused. They judged Mengistu as they judged themselves, expecting him to play by the rules of their democratic "game." When he pretended to submit to the will of the majority, they believed him. Some counseled caution, and argued that Mengistu should be arrested, but to no avail. "Isn't he our comrade-in-arms? Hasn't he risked his life for us?" In the meantime, Mengistu was laying low, pretending to abide by the more collegial form of government, biding his time. On February 2, 1977, he sprang his trap: the faction members were accused of being "imperialist agents," and Teferi Banti and all the leading members of the Dergue opposition were killed at a shootout in the Menelik palace. The democratic revolution was over. Mengistu assumed full dictatorial powers—and the Soviet leadership compared Mengistu's triumph to the Bolshevik revolution!

**Phase III: Mengistu and the "Red Terror"**

The "Red terror" that followed was the final betrayal of the Ethiopian revolution. It is estimated that over 5,000 Ethiopian youth between the ages of 12 and 25 perished between December 1977 and February 1978. The ranks of the EPRP were drastically depleted, and what was left of the membership demoralized by splits and recriminations. Its few remaining urban guerrillas splintered into two factions, with the "Bolsheviks" advocating protracted war in the countryside, and a smaller faction favoring continued urban warfare. A few later joined the Dergue and formed an "unholy alliance" with the MEISON leftovers.

Parts of the terror campaign were organized and directed with the help of MEISON. This leads to questions about the MEISON membership in particular, and the role of terror in a revolutionary situation in general. Leaving aside zealots and "lumpen" hired hands, could and did MEISON members distinguish between pure terror and the revolutionary process, or were they themselves terrorized into supporting it? More generally, is terror an essential part of any revolution? The words "terror" and "terrorist" are nowadays associated with armed rebel groups that operate clandestinely against an established government. In most cases, this is done for a cause, or as a result of a sense of injustice. The established governments call these people terrorists, while they themselves use other names. Yet the violence used by the Dergue must be clearly distinguished from the legitimate use of revolutionary violence, which is, in contrast, rationally organized, purposeful, and controlled by a party that represents the great mass of the people. This was the sense in which Marx saw revolutionary violence as the midwife of history, the instrument of an ascendant class struggling to replace an old order and usher in a new era. It thus has a revolutionary legitimacy, and its use must be in the context of a coherent revolutionary theory; it cannot proceed on the basis of the whims of a dictator, military or otherwise.

In Ethiopia, terror has been officially and openly used by the regime in power, and has been justified as an instrument of class struggle—the media in Ethiopia often talk of the masses "drawing the revolutionary sword to smite all counter-revolutionaries and enemies of the masses"—so that it has become confused with revolutionary process. The powerholders try to justify it in terms of the exigencies of class struggle, as a "necessary evil." Bourgeois social scientists, taking the powerholders' claim to Marxism at its face value, then wistfully ask: "What price Marxism?" But no amount of rhetoric can change reality: the Ethiopian masses remain ill-organized, frightened, and confused. Class struggle has very little to do with it.

This sort of terror can only be seen as a morbid expression of the corruption of power, as the following examples of its excesses should amply demonstrate. For the Dergue, killing "anarchists" was not enough; their bodies had to be desecrated and left lying in the streets with placards saying "Anarchist" or "Enemy of the people" stuck on them. Relatives were forbidden to take the bodies for customary burial, and any display of grief was forbidden on pain of arrest and possible execution. Young children of the people arrested or killed were left without care, and their neighbors, who would customarily have taken them temporarily, were forbidden to do so. The fate of children was not even openly discussed—people whispered about it in the night.

"Confession" or "self-criticism" was also used. All the adult residents in a neighborhood, or *kebele*'s jurisdiction (there are 528 *kebeles* in Addis Ababa, with roughly 3,000 residents in each) were summoned to a meeting in a public place, and the names of four or five people—usually suspected "anarchists" who had already "confessed"—were then read out from a prepared list. The captive audience was told that the list contained names of more "anarchists" or "enemies of the people" who were present at the meeting, and leniency was promised to those who voluntarily confessed. In fact, of course, there were no other names, but people were nevertheless induced to "confess" all kinds of sins, many of which they had never committed. And few of the victims ever received the promised leniency.

The military and the *kebele*'s militia periodically carried out raids of government offices and private homes, in all the cities, especially Addis Ababa, in search of weapons and "counter-revolutionaries." Any resistance led to the shooting of the suspect. In one instance, Girma Kebede, an excessively zealous *kebele* leader and MEISON member arrested Mengistu's uncle, Asrat Wolde, together with other officials of the ministry of education. He, however, survived to tell Mengistu, who thereupon ordered the execution of Girma, along with some of his co-workers, who were hanged with him as cover-up. Those executed, and most particularly their leader, had been highly commended for their zealous prosecution of the war against the "anarchists." MEISON protested the fate of the *kebele* chief, but to no avail.

The Red terror has been tragic testimony to a revolution gone astray under a leadership heady with its own power. Whatever positive results there may have been from early reforms have been negated by the crippling effects of the terror campaign, as both life and work lost all meaning. Equally devastating for the future course of the revolution, in the minds of the Ethiopian people terror has become associated with "socialist revolution." And the habitual and massive use of violence cannot stop, for the regime's survival now depends on it.

The Dergue had proclaimed itself the creator of the "democratic revolution," and yet it did not take long for its anti-democratic nature to be revealed. This raises the question of whether a democratic dialogue and united front among the various left groups was ever possible, and whether an organization such as the Dergue is capable of responding to a democratic challenge with other than repression and terror. Some commentators explain the Dergue's anti-democratic behavior by pointing to the autocratic nature of its leader, Mengistu. But while Mengistu's role has been important, to explain the Dergue's actions in so simple a manner is to miss the overriding importance of the feudo-imperial legacy of the Ethiopian state, which is deeply engrained not only in the consciousness of its ruling class, but of all aspirants to power. Thus while to the casual observer the land reform proclamation might have appeared to have dealt a final blow to feudalism, feudal values and methods that have existed for centuries are not so easily destroyed. They may be disguised by slogans and programs, but they are institutionalized in a military structure that places obedience to a superior above all else, and in autocratic behavior on the part of individuals and groups, including not only the military but members of the Ethiopian left as well.

The Dergue could not tolerate any group that threatened its power, and, as we have seen, it either attacked them or tried to absorb them. It was aided enormously by the failure of the two main left groups to work together, and this led to the Dergue/ MEISON alliance, which effectively put an end to the possibility of a democratic revolution. While it lasted, this alliance served several purposes for the Dergue in its attempt to do away with the EPRP. First, it seemed to lend the Dergue additional revolutionary legitimacy through its association with a civilian group. Second, MEISON gave the Dergue the ideological and political support it needed to counter the EPRP's growing popularity (*Democracia*, for instance, at one point had a larger circulation than the government newspapers). Third, MEISON members could provide critical information about the EPRP's "weak points," because leaders of both groups had known each other as students a few years back. Fourth, the Dergue was able to use MEISON to undo the work of the ZEMECHA campaign in organizing the peasants. The military was persuaded by MEISON to keep the peasant associations, but to drain them of their democratic essence and turn them into vehicles for communicating the commands of the rulers. And finally, the verbal warfare between MEISON and the EPRP, skillfully managed by the Dergue, led the EPRP to change its tactics and focus on urban guerrilla warfare.

It was this fifth service rendered by MEISON—and abetted by the EPRP—that set the Ethiopian revolution on a counterrevolutionary course. It enabled the Dergue to divert attention from its failure to institute democratic processes, and use violence to suppress democratic demands and opposition to its rule.

MEISON's alliance with the Dergue was only temporary, however. As MEISON appeared to pose an increasing challenge to the power of the Dergue, Mengistu announced the formation of his own party, called SEDED, in the spring of 1976, and became a Marxist-Leninist overnight. Even the devil, as they say in Christian circles, could quote the scripture to his purpose. SEDED was composed primarily of military cadre beholden to Mengistu, and was clearly designed to reinforce the power of a Dergue that he would lead. The creation of SEDED reflected Mengistu's growing personal dictatorial powers.

The Dergue/MEISON rivalry was at first carried on behind the scenes, and only came into the open when Mengistu ordered the execution of Girma Kebede. When MEISON had protested, Mengistu used SEDED, along with the military, to watch the activities of prominent MEISON members and challenge their methods of recruitment of *kebele* members. The strategy was to terrorize them, splitting the organization, and included some assassinations. Some of the deaths were attributed to the EPRP urban guerrillas, but are believed to have been the work of SEDED.

When the MEISON leadership saw the futility of continuing the alliance in the face of this threat of elimination, they decided to try a coup. They conceived a plan to recruit the militia from areas around Addis Ababa, take the barracks by surprise, and seize power in the ensuing chaos. The outcome was to be expected: when the coup failed, the MEISON leadership ran in disarray. MEISON chairman Kebede Menguesha and his little band of followers escaped to the Selale district north of Addis Ababa, where they were surrounded and killed while resisting capture. Haile Fida, chairman of the politbureau, was caught in Addis Ababa, along with many other leaders. The MEISON movement was literally decapitated.

By the end of 1977, the Ethiopian left, as represented by the EPRP and MEISON, was in complete disarray. SEDED recruited many among the remaining members of MEISON, through coercion and intimidation. The EPRP's division into two sections, the "Bolsheviks" and the "Mensheviks," weakened it. The Bolshevik faction advocated a protracted people's war based in the countryside, whereas the other faction stuck to urban guerrilla tactics, despite their failure in 1976–1977. Many disillusioned EPRP members joined SEDED, while others left the country altogether. A few persisted, girding themselves for a long war. As will be seen in Chapter 4, the EPRP army, which was stationed in Tigray, was involved in a deadly contradiction with the Tigray People's Liberation Front (TPLF). Hundreds of

EPRP fighters left the field, disgusted with what they considered to be an ill-prepared and ill-conceived campaign. Some joined the "Bolsheviks," who had come to start a guerrilla base in the mountains around Gondar.

The attitude of the Ethiopian left to the Eritrean liberation struggle and to the national question has been confused at best, and deceptive at worst. On the whole, the EPRP's position came closest to recognizing the right of the Eritrean people to independence, but stopped short of accepting that the Eritrean question is a colonial one. As regards the national question, be it in Tigray, the Ogaden, or among the Oromo, the left has an equally poor record. The EPRP position, despite the progressive stand taken by some student supporters and a few members, has been negative, and in the case of Tigray counter-revolutionary, as we will see in more detail later. MEISON has supported the national question rhetorically, but failed to support any national group in its demand for self-determination. The Ogaden case was an acid test, and one which MEISON failed.

## Mengistu and His Party

The Dergue's divisive and manipulative skills helped destroy the civilian left factions, while its cooptive skills helped it "acquire" the ideas and organizational structure built by MEISON. Meanwhile, it was organizing SEDED, which swallowed the allied groups in July 1979 and was expected to metamorphose into a new Ethiopian Workers' Party the following September, the first anniversary of the emperor's overthrow.

The fate of Mengistu's "party," and of the war in Eritrea, have been curiously connected. The announcement of the new "party" had been expected for two years, and was expected to coincide with the end of the Eritrean "rebellion"; instead, between August 1978 and July 1979 the Dergue lost a third of its army in Eritrea. But the question of the "party" could no longer be postponed, and so Mengistu adopted a two-stage plan, the first stage of which was the appointment of a commission to organize the establishment of a party. The commission was to be the only body legally empowered to organize a party, and the party, once established, was to replace the Dergue. The second stage would occur when the commission selected the members of the future party.

What Mengistu seems to be doing is attempting to create a party loyal to himself and to the military group he leads. The commission is composed primarily of military cadre, many of whom were members of SEDED, and there seems to be no plan to widen the membership to include civilians, including former MEISON cadre. When asked about this, Mengistu responded: "These people who betrayed us . . . cannot be considered as possible members." At the same time, the phasing out of the Dergue is not expected to create problems for Mengistu since half its members already hold powerful provincial and other executive positions.

Paradoxically, Mengistu is not an accepted member of the Amhara ruling nation, which makes his ascent to imperial power a matter of great fascination. He has surprised everyone, including those who helped him up the ladder of power—some of whom have been surprised to their graves. The final victims of his surprise may well be his Soviet backers, who have already quarreled with his methods of establishing his party. But although tensions are there—and a new party that the Russians cannot control will only add to them—the Ethiopian dependence on the Soviet Union for arms is too great for any immediate falling-out. On the one hand, Mengistu will try to build a more solid base of support, independent of external and internal forces. Yet on the other hand, by using the rhetoric of a workers' party, he may be taken at his word by some "true believers"—particularly those influenced by Soviet-trained cadre—and fashion an instrument that will lead to his demise. It would not be the first time, and events in Afghanistan and elsewhere must weigh heavily on his mind. Uneasy lies the head that wears the crown, even if it has a red star stuck on it.

# 3

## Eritrea:
## A Forgotten Colonial Struggle

### Early History

Eritrea has an area of approximately 119,000 sq. km. and a population of over 3.5 million. It stretches for some 800 km. along the Red Sea coast and is bordered in the north and west by the Sudan, and on the south by Ethiopia and Djibouti. It is divided into the central and northern highlands, the western plains of Barka with their rich soils, and the arid eastern Afar region, sometimes known as the Danakil plain. Climatically, at Massawa on the Red Sea coast the temperature reaches over 38°C in the summer, while in the plateaus of Hamasien, Seraie, Akule-Guzai, and parts of Senhit, the summer is rainy and cool. It is hot again on the plains of Barka, although less humid than on the coast.

The contrasting geographical features and climatic conditions have led to the development of different patterns of economic and social life. The people of the coastal region, of parts of Senhit and Sahel, and of the plains of Barka share a pastoral way of life, the Tigre language, and the Muslim religion. Only a small minority have been drawn into plantation agriculture, owned and run by foreign concerns. The highland Eritreans, on the other hand, are predominantly settled cultivators who raise such staple foods as wheat, barley, sorghum, maize, and taff (a fine local grain). They share their culture, Tigrinya language, and Christian religion with the people of Tigray to the south.

Eritrea has long been a region of colonization. The early inhabitants of the area, a Nilotic people, were displaced or absorbed by the Hamitic people, who came from the north. Then, between 1000 and 400 B.C., more colonizers migrated peacefully across the Red Sea and occupied the coastal areas, moving gradually up into the highlands, where they found the climate more hospitable. Still other colonizers came as conquerors. All were eventually absorbed by the more numerous Hamitic people, who also absorbed the technological skills of the immigrants. By 300 A.D., the greater part of Eritrea, as well as Tigray, formed the central region of the Christian Axumite empire, which at its height stretched south to the northern edge of the Simien mountains and northwest to Nubia, in present-day Sudan. Axum thrived on its maritime trade, carried out through the ancient port of Adulis, near Massawa. But with the rise of Islam and the occupation of the Red Sea coast by Arabs in 640 A.D., external trade declined. Internal political dissension and the incursion of Bejas from the north furthered the decline of the empire, which finally fell at the end of the ninth century.[1] Western Eritrea, which was not part of the Axumite empire, was also the subject of repeated invasion by neighboring nations, while some of its residents crossed over to the Sudan.

From the fall of the Axumite empire until the end of the thirteenth century, the Bejas ruled the highlands. Meanwhile, the Amhara kingdom, which flourished further south after the fall of Axum, established an empire centered in the mountain fastnesses of Wallo, Manz, and Gondar. It was not until the fifteenth century that the Amharas, who came to be known as Abyssinians, were able to establish a tenuous rule over the Eritrean highlands—tenuous because the people, geographically isolated and unaccustomed to outside rule, were fiercely nationalistic and stubbornly resisted Abyssinian attempts to rule them. Distance and ecology (a semi-arid zone) similarly enabled them to resist attempts at colonization from the Sudan to the west. But on both fronts, the peoples, when not at war, traded and learned from each other through critical mountain passes.

The rise of Islam, followed by the advent of the Ottoman Turks, critically affected the entire region. The Ottomans occu-

pied the Red Sea coast in 1557, and although they did not penetrate the highlands, they effectively cut them off from the outside world. The central Eritrean highlanders and neighboring northern Abyssinians sometimes worked together to resist alien incursion, but this cooperation was often undermined by the Abyssinian ambition to expand into Eritrea. The Orthodox church of Abyssinia, under the Egyptian Coptic church, aided in the attempt to forge a highland Christian kingdom united against Islamic Turkish rule.

In 1872, after over three hundred years of Turkish hegemony, Egypt made a bid to succeed the Ottomans as a regional power, and as a first step attempted to do what the Turks had failed to do: gain control of the highlands. With British help, the Egyptians won the transfer of all Turkish possessions in Eritrea through a treaty in 1875. Spurred on by the success of this diplomatic coup, they then attempted to expand and secure their gains militarily, only to be defeated by the Eritreans and their Tigrean allies in a series of battles west of Massawa.

The British motive for setting Egypt on such an adventure stemmed from a desire to keep the French out of the area, which, since the opening of the Suez Canal in 1869, had become strategically vital. Egypt was also junior partner with England in a condominium over the Sudan, although this arrangement was overthrown in 1881, when the Mahdist revolt led to the establishment of the Mahdist state, which lasted until 1898.[2] It was at this time that Eritrea came under Italian colonial rule, the specific events of which will be discussed in more detail below.

The Eritrean people's sense of entrapment and isolation, as succeeding colonial powers either encircled them or occupied their land, lies at the root of Eritrean nationalism and a fierce spirit of independence. It is not a new phenomenon; it has its history in the struggle of the Eritrean people against repeated attempts to overthrow alien rule.

### Italian Colonial Rule, 1889–1941

The factors that emerged following the opening of the canal, as well as a desire for colonial possessions, brought Italy to the area. Its desire was facilitated by the Anglo-French rivalry: the British wanted to exclude the French, who had already occupied Djibouti, from the region. (Djibouti lies at the entrance to the Red Sea, opposite the British-held port of Aden, and thus controls the access to the Bab el Mandeb) without which control of the canal itself is incomplete.)The French, on the other hand, wanted to link their western African possessions to the Indian Ocean—a response to Britain's Cape to Cairo dream.

It was at this historical point that Italy began its move into the area. In 1869 the Rubattino Shipping Company fraudulently purchased an area of the port of Assab, and the Italian government took over the entire port in 1882 and declared it a protectorate.

Then, with British collusion, the Italians occupied Massawa in 1885 and began to push into the interior.

The trail was coated with the blood of thousands of Italian soldiers as the Eritreans and their Tigrean allies fought and defeated the Italian army at Saati and Dogali. Nevertheless, by 1889 all of Eritrea had been occupied, and Menelik had signed the Treaty of Ucciali, under which he recognized Italian rule over Eritrea.[3] He was, at the same time, engaged in the conquest of Oromo, Wolamo, Gurage, and other nations to the south and west and the Somali to the east, covering a much larger and richer area.

Having secured a firm foothold in Eritrea, and having tasted the first fruits of success, the Italians' appetite for dominions and wealth drove them on toward Ethiopia. In 1896, however, the Italian army suffered a crushing defeat at Adwa at the hands of Menelik's army, well-armed and provisioned and backed by the wealth of the plundered peoples of the south. At this point Menelik could have chosen to drive the Italians into the sea and occupy the coast himself; he chose instead to preserve his newly created empire to the south and stopped at the 1889 treaty line. By so doing, he in effect once again recognized Italian colonial rule over Eritrea.

Two different imperial territories now existed side by side, one governed by an African imperial power, the other by white European colonial power. Both forced their language and political culture on the conquered people, and so the consequences would appear to have been the same. But there was an essential difference, one that would have significantly different results. While Menelik's Ethiopia was a feudal state that placed a feudal ruling class over its conquered peoples, as we saw in Chapter 1, Italy was a budding bourgeois nation-state that had taken its place among the community of European nations a few decades earlier. Thus although both exploited a conquered people and their wealth, their methods were based on different modes of production—one feudal, the other capitalist. As might therefore be expected, each produced a different social and political awareness among its subjected peoples.

The Italians exploited Eritrea for profit, and developed a market-based, capitalist economy that was both a place for settlers and a market for Italian manufacturers. The details of how this developed can be gleaned from the reports of Ferdinando Martini, the most celebrated Italian governor-general of Eritrea. He shows not only the primacy of the profit motive, but also the haste with which the Italians sought to make up for the time they felt they had lost as late arrivers in the colonial scramble for Africa.

From the Eritrean's point of view, the Italian settlement policy was the most dramatic aspect of the colonial experience. It called for the takeover of land, either forcibly or through the introduction of changes in the land tenure system. Vast areas of fertile lowland plain, as well as all land adjoining rivers, were expropriated and declared "state domain," and then distributed to Italian settlers, who were aided in starting commercial farms— a pattern familiar to other settler-colonies, including Kenya and Rhodesia (Zimbabwe).

At the same time, thousands were driven from their only means of livelihood and forced to sell their labor power. They thus became a cheap labor force on the commercial farms, for building and operating the colonial infrastructure, and, later, in manufacturing and service industries. A railway was built to link Massawa, Asmara, Keren, and Agordat, as were roads that ran the length and breadth of the country. As the different areas became linked, and as the labor force was pushed off its land, an Eritrean working class gradually emerged.

With the rise of fascism in Italy, and Mussolini's decision to invade Ethiopia in 1935, massive investment transformed Eritrea's economy. The preparations for the war against Ethiopia led to the extension of the port facilities at Massawa; the construction of the world's longest aerial ropeway, from Massawa to Asmara, to handle massive shipments of equipment and supplies; the construction of a strategic north-to-south road; and the rebuilding of the airports at Asmara and Gura.

This process of rapid growth was accompanied by even more rapid urbanization. The population of Asmara increased sixfold, with the indigenous population rising from 15,000 in 1935 to 90,000 in 1941. The main urban centers—Dekemhare, Agordat, Tessenei, Assab, Adi Caieh, Adi Ugri, Ghinda, and Nefasit—

were expanded at this point, and by 1940 about 20 percent of the population was living in cities.[4] Eritrea had one of Africa's largest urban working classes, in absolute as well as relative terms. It also had a colonial bourgeoisie, rigidly separated along both class and racial lines, and living in segregated residential areas.

Italian colonial rule, like all colonial rule, was marked by the absence of educational and other policies designed for the benefit of the indigenous population. What education there was existed in order to produce a subclerical servant class, and had the fifth grade as the terminal point. Students were made to sing about the glory of Italy; they had to depend on the oral tales told by their elders to maintain their pride in their own history. The only Eritreans who participated in national affairs were a few carefully selected notables who were appointed to act as liaisons between colonizers and colonized. The mass of Eritreans were left in the remaining rural areas, or marginalized in a subproletarian and subhuman existence in the cities. Hideous shantytowns mushroomed on the outskirts of Asmara, in sharp contrast to the beautiful mansions of the Italian residents, who flaunted their newly acquired wealth—a contrast that only served to enhance the Eritreans' class consciousness and was added to the suppressed national struggle.

In 1935 Mussolini, encouraged by Italian capitalists determined to acquire overseas markets, raw materials, and cheap labor, and with the defeat at Adwa still fresh in his mind, invaded Ethiopia. Eritreans were again used as cannon fodder by the Italian colonial army, as they had been in Libya, Somalia, and at Adwa. But returning soldiers were to bring back information about the world around them, and about the nature and purpose of colonial rule. Thousands even crossed over to the Ethiopian side and turned their guns against the common colonizer. Many were martyred alongside their Ethiopian brothers. All these experiences contributed to the increased political awareness of the Eritrean people.

Five years later Mussolini decided to back Hitler in World War II. That fateful decision brought the British into Eritrea when Keren fell to them in March 1941. Italian soldiers fled by the thousands, creating a fugitive army, its members no better than the people they had exploited for half a century.

## British Colonial Rule, 1941–1952

Before the outbreak of World War II, the British promised to help the Eritreans exercise their right to self-determination if they would help defeat the Italians. The British Royal Air Force dropped leaflets during the hostilities promising freedom to Eritrea and stimulating nationalist aspirations. The political agitation grew in intensity, and the British were welcomed as liberators.

It gradually became clear, however, that the British would not honor their pledge and political agitation began to take on a more organized and militant form. This was possible because the British permitted a measure of freedom of speech and association, and had established a press and information service that broadcast news on the progress of the war in Europe and other events in English, Tigrinya, and Arabic. A group of political activists and commentators developed, some of whom were to play important roles in the Eritrean national struggle. The most celebrated among them was Wolde-Ab Wolde-Mariam, whose column commenting on Eritrea's future was read and reread, discussed and debated, in the cities and large villages. It played an enormously important role in galvanizing mass political opinion, especially in the urban centers, and in helping to raise the awareness of the Eritrean people. At the same time, schools were mushrooming in the cities and villages, under a crash program directed by an energetic British education officer. These rapidly produced literate youngsters who helped in the spread of political education by reading newspaper articles to their parents.

By the end of 1945 this political activity had crystallized into three political "parties"—the Eritrean Independence Party, led by Wolde-Ab; the Rabita Al-Islamia, or Islamic League Party, led by Ibrahim Sultan Ali; and the Unionist Party, led by Tedla Bairu.

At the Paris peace conference in June 1946, Italy formally renounced its right to Libya, Eritrea, and Italian Somaliland, whose disposal was to be determined by agreement among France, Great Britain, the United States, and the Soviet Union. If they could not agree within a year, the matter was to be submitted to the United Nations.[5] In November 1947, a commission of inquiry was established to visit the three territories and report on the political situation. The commission submitted its report in May 1948, but the four powers could not agree, and the matter was therefore presented to the third session of the United Nations in April 1949. The UN considered the Bevin-Sforza plan, which divided Libya into three parts, each to be placed under "trusteeship"—one to the British, one to the French, and one to the Italians—with Italian Somaliland to be administered under an Italian trusteeship, and Eritrea to be partitioned: the highland and Red Sea coast to Ethiopia, with the western plains to be united with the Sudan (at that time ruled by the British). The whole scheme collapsed, however, and it was not until the fourth session that the future of Libya and Italian Somaliland was decided. Libya was to be granted its independence by January 1952 and Somaliland was to be placed under a ten-year Italian trusteeship, after which it too would become independent. There was no agreement on Eritrea, and a second commission of inquiry, composed of representatives from Burma, Guatemala, Norway, Pakistan, and South Africa, was created.[6]

This commission presented its findings on June 28, 1949. It opposed partition—an accurate, if partial, reflection of Eritrean sentiment—but this was the only matter on which the Eritrean people's views were represented. Despite emphatic and unequivocal demands for independence expressed both before the commission and in petitions, demonstrations, strikes, and so on, the majority, consisting of Burma, Norway, and South Africa, recommended a close association of Eritrea with Ethiopia; Burma and South Africa, however, proposed federation with Ethiopia under Ethiopian sovereignty, while Norway recommended unconditional union. Guatemala and Pakistan, in a minority report, recommended a ten-year UN trusteeship, followed by independence. The majority report concluded, for example, that

Eritrea was incapable of establishing a viable economy, a conclusion that flies in the face of the facts and was influenced by
the opinions of the "administering power," which controlled all
economic data.

The debate on the second commission of inquiry's report took
place at the beginning of the Korean war. The United States had
emerged as the dominant economic and military power after
World War II, and was fast replacing Britain in many areas of the
world. The United States and its allies favored a "federal" solution, and only the Soviet Union and nine other nations favored
complete independence. United Nations Resolution 390 A (v),
passed on December 2, 1950, thus constituted Eritrea an autonomous unit to be federated with Ethiopia under the sovereignty of
the Ethiopian crown. This was clearly not only in violation of
the UN Charter, but was contrary to the wishes of the Eritrean
people for self-determination.[7]

The preamble to the resolution reads:

> Taking into consideration (a) the wishes and welfare of the in-
> habitants of Eritrea, including the views of the various racial,
> religious, and political groups of the provinces of the territory and
> the capacity of the people for self-government; (b) the interests of
> peace and security in East Africa; (c) the rights and claims of
> Ethiopia based on geographical historical, ethnic, or economic
> reasons, including in particular Ethiopia's legitimate need for
> adequate access to the sea. . . . Desiring that this association [of
> Eritrea with Ethiopia] assures to the inhabitants of Eritrea the
> *fullest respect and safeguards for their institutions, traditions,*
> *religions, and languages,* as well as the widest possible measure
> of self-government. (Emphasis added.)

The inconsistencies inherent in this legal jargon are evident.
How can the "interests of peace" be secured when a basic
condition has been denied: the exercise of the right of self-
determination, which the United Nations instead took unto
itself? How could a world tribunal that took into consideration
the "wishes and welfare of the inhabitants of Eritrea" arrive at a
decision that denied those very wishes? Was it necessary to
fabricate (or to endorse the Ethiopian fabrication of) "historical
reasons" in order to advance the economic interests of Ethiopia?

Was Ethiopia's "legitimate" need for adequate access to the sea in itself sufficient to lead to the denial of the right of self-determination to the Eritrean people? Ethiopia is not, after all, the only nation that has a need for access to the sea.

The real reasons, of course, lie elsewhere. John Foster Dulles, then U.S. Secretary of State, stated these bluntly in a speech before the UN Security Council in 1952:

> From the point of view of justice, the opinions of the Eritrean people must receive consideration. Nevertheless, the strategic interest of the United States in the Red Sea basin and considerations of security and world peace make it necessary that the country has to be linked with our ally, Ethiopia.[8]

The phrasing of Dulles' statement is significant. The word "nevertheless," coming as it does after the sentence that recognizes the rights of the Eritrean people, reveals beyond doubt that the United States (and hence the United Nations) knew the wishes of the Eritrean people to be decisively for independence. The unqualified wish of the Eritrean people is juxtaposed to U.S. imperialist interests and those of its newfound ally.

Aklilu Habte Wold, Ethiopian minister of foreign affairs at the time, has since claimed that Haile Selassie had openly placed Ethiopia on the side of Western powers, led by the United States, in return for this "deal" on Eritrea.[9] And indeed, Ethiopia's commitment to the United States was fulfilled in more ways than one. Haile Selassie sent a battalion of his well-trained Imperial Bodyguard to fight on the U.S. side in the Korean war, while the United States and Ethiopia signed a secret, twenty-five-year mutual defense pact whereby the United States "leased" the Kagnew base and Haile Selassie was granted military and other assistance.[10]

## From Federation to Annexation, 1952–1962

The United Nations resolution provided for an autonomous Eritrean government with legislative, executive, and judicial authority over its own domestic affairs, while matters of defense, foreign affairs, currency and finance, foreign and interstate trade, and communications were to be under "federal" (read: Ethiopian) jurisdiction. In the interim period, between December 1950 and September 1952, Anze Matienzo, a Bolivian diplomat, who had been appointed United Nations commissioner, was to prepare and submit a draft constitution to an Eritrean assembly to be convened by the British administering authority. Matienzo spent many weeks negotiating the draft constitution with the emperor and members of his government. The chief difficulty was developing a bourgeois-democratic constitution for a semi-feudal autocracy, a difficulty Matienzo proposed to solve simply by adding some "democratic" provisions to the 1931 constitution. But this was not easy because of the higher degree of political and democratic development of Eritrea, which somehow had to be forcibly wedded to the feudal autocracy. Perhaps recognizing the problem, Matienzo added this paragraph to his final report, citing juristic opinion as authority:

> It does not follow that the United Nations would no longer have any right to deal with the question. *The United Nations Resolution on Eritrea would remain an international instrument and, if violated, the General Assembly could be seized of the matter.*[11] (Emphasis added.)

Matienzo's cautionary remarks might be seen as prophetic, but for the fact that he had a clear sense of the emperor's annexationist ambitions, and had heard petitions from Eritreans who had been the object of Ethiopian smear campaigns and terrorist acts.

The emperor was represented in Eritrea by Andargachew Mesai, whose role was supposed to be primarily symbolic: he was to promulgate legislation and read imperial speeches or messages, and the only substantive legal power he had was his right to return to the Eritrean assembly legislation that he considered encroached on federal (Ethiopian) jurisdiction. But Andargachew saw his role as being much more than that, and, with the emperor's backing, he set out to undermine the democratic principles of the Eritrean constitution and bring the Eritrean government under his control. He made this imperial intention explicit in a speech to the Eritrean assembly on March 22, 1955:

There are no internal or external affairs, as far as the Office of His Imperial Majesty's Representative is concerned, and there will be none in the future. The affairs of Eritrea concern Ethiopia as a whole and the Emperor.

The Eritrean government was headed by Tedla Bairu, a member of the pro-Ethiopian Unionist Party. Once installed as chief executive, he was at loggerheads with Andargachew as he attempted to resist Andargachew's encroachment on his jurisdiction, both in the political and the economic domains. The paradoxical dilemma of a democratically elected chief executive being subverted by the representative of a feudal autocracy was eventually resolved when Tedla resigned, followed by the president of the assembly.[12] At the same time, the Eritrean attorney-general (a British national) was engaged in a series of futile legal battles in the "federal" courts in a parallel effort to check the encroachment.

Andargachew replaced Tedla with Asfaha Wolde-Mikael, a more trusted Unionist and a faithful servant of the Italian colonial rulers. Asfaha began to dismantle the remaining independent institutions of Eritrea by placing Unionist cronies in key positions throughout the administration. The legislative assembly was controlled by another Unionist, an orthodox cleric named Dimetros Gebre Mariam. These two, under the direction of Andargachew and with the active help of the police force, used a preventive detention law systemically to terrorize the people into submission. Protesters were jailed or sent into exile.

At the same time Andargachew entered into a number of joint ventures with foreign and local businessmen, mostly in the service industries and transport, and thus presided over the rise of a new bourgeoisie that began to play an important role in running Eritrea's economy. This small but powerful bourgeoisie formed the nucleus of a large number of collaborators who were given government positions, land grants, or other inducements—all with the emperor's blessing.

These activities imposed severe economic and social strains on the Eritrean people. At the same time, a few key industries were closed and moved to Addis Ababa—their foreign owners instructed to make the move or have their property confiscated.

The aim was twofold: first, to weaken Eritrea economically and then prove (retroactively) that its economy was not viable; and second, to strike at the labor force, which had been organized and effective at the national level since the 1950s. Thousands did leave to seek work elsewhere, but this failed to break the backbone of organized labor.

The continued violations of democratic rights led to sporadic protest. This internal process was aided by broadcasts made by exiled opposition leaders, notably Wolde-Ab. In 1956 he began daily broadcasts from Cairo that lasted for a few months and fanned the nationalist embers that lay buried beneath the ashes of police intimidation. The protests began taking more organized form. Throughout 1956 students intermittently boycotted classes and in 1957, when Tigrinya and Arabic were replaced by Amharic as the official language, they took to the streets. The imposition of Amharic not only expressly violated a provision of the UN resolution,[13] but it imposed a painful obstacle in the path of the Eritrean children—the effects of which were felt when countless numbers failed the secondary and university entrance examinations and were then effectively denied higher education.

Haile Selassie was able to stop Wolde-Ab's broadcasts by backing Nasser's bid to nationalize the Suez Canal in 1956, but the message had been delivered loud and clear—and in a language that everyone understood and could remember.[14]

In 1958 the trade unions, which had been officially banned, called a general strike. The strike and the accompanying demonstrations were clear proof of the Eritrean will to resist the dismantling of their democratic rights. Asfaha ordered the police to fire on demonstrators, killing and wounding over five hundred. That brutal act cast the die for a change in the form of the Eritrean struggle, from open protest to underground operation.

It was in this climate that the Eritrean Liberation Movement (ELM) was born. Students, workers, and intellectuals created it, and dedicated men like Wolde-Ab gave it inspiration and instruction in its early stages. It had two principal centers: one was in the highlands, centered in Asmara and other urban centers, and the other was in the lowlands and among exiled Eritreans living in the Sudan. The highland group came to be known as Mahber Shewate (the Committee of Seven), while the lowland group was known as Harakat'atahrir Al-Eritrea (Eritrean Liberation Movement), or simply Haraka. The two were in contact—including through sports and other activities—but were not organizationally linked. Their principal activities were aimed at organizing resistance among Eritrean workers, intellectuals, students, and small traders by raising funds, and writing, mimeographing, and distributing leaflets. Their activities had not gone further than the leaflet stage when the police struck.

The movement was unable to carry out any systematic struggle against the state's reign of terror and was quickly decapitated in a series of raids. By November 1962, the ELM was no longer a viable underground organization, although isolated cells remained, printing and distributing leaflets. Yet it had carried the national struggle one stage further, and had prepared the way for a protracted and popularly based armed struggle organized in the countryside by showing the Eritrean people that any other, more peaceful, form of resistance was impossible.

Then, on November 14, 1962, Haile Selassie annexed Eritrea—with the tacit support of the United States and without a murmur being heard in the United Nations. The mechanics were simple: the Eritrean assembly—many of whose members by this time were virtually handpicked—was pressured into accepting a speech from the throne that announced that the federation was dissolved. The assembly was surrounded by units of armed forces and police, and there were machine guns inside the building when the "vote" was taken. Those who stayed away, or walked out in protest, were arrested and beaten. Tedla Ogbit, the Eritrean chief of police who was instrumental in this campaign of intimidation, was subsequently rewarded with a gold watch from the emperor and a special hand gun. (His later reward was his own death, which the media called suicide; the truth is that he had come to realize the crime he had committed against his own people, and had started expressing his regrets and sharing plans for a revolt when he was betrayed and executed.)

The emperor then proceeded to replace Eritrean laws and institutions with Ethiopian ones—an act that surpassed even the colonial interference of the Italians, who had at least left local laws and customs alone. The Ethiopian army of occupation was bolstered with United States and Israeli help, and dispersed throughout Eritrea.

## The Eritrean Liberation Front, 1961–1969

It should be clear by now that the Eritrean question is a *colonial* question, not an issue of secession. In terms of international law, Ethiopia's repeated violations of the UN resolution—and the UN's refusal to heed repeated Eritrean pleas to be heard—have given the Eritrean people the right to use any and every means available to wage a struggle against an occupying power.

At the same time, the Eritrean struggle is an anti-imperialist struggle, for Haile Selassie's alliance with the United States, his military and economic dependence on it, and the United States' tacit support of his colonialist ambitions have turned Ethiopia into a neo-colony and thus brought the entire question into the realm of international politics. The move to the stage of armed struggle must therefore be seen as a final stage after all peaceful means of protest were exhausted, and its subsequent course must be seen in the light of this larger situation.

The specific impetus to launch the Eritrean Liberation Front (ELF) came from some of the older Eritrean leaders living in exile in Cairo, particularly Idris Mohammed Adam, former president of the Eritrean assembly, and Ibrahim Sultan Ali, secretary-general of the Islamic League Party. Their individual attempts, and those of others like Wolde-Ab to petition the United Nations had proved futile, and the primary aim in founding the ELF was to create an organization through which they could pressure the United Nations for support. They had little understanding of the way in which the United States dominated the organization.

When Idris and Ibrahim visited Saudi Arabia in 1960, the Eritrean community there had called upon them to form an organization and start the armed struggle. Exiled Eritreans in other Arab countries, and in particular the active student body in Cairo, had made similar calls, inspired in part by the example of the Algerian war of liberation. When Idris returned to Cairo, he announced the establishment of the ELF, only to be beset by claims of prior legitimacy by some of the exiled leaders of the ELM. It was amid such factionalism that Ahmed Idris Awate, an Eritrean who had been an NCO in the Sudanese army and a "rebel" opposing British rule in Eritrea, declared the beginning of armed struggle in the western lowlands. His guerrilla army included other Eritreans who had also been soldiers or NCO's in the Sudanese army. Idris Mohammed Adam's group endorsed Awate's decision and decided to send him supplies.

Awate died in the middle of 1962, but his liberation army continued to grow. By mid-1964, when the first foreign assistance came from Syria in the form of twenty Kalashnikov assault rifles, it had 250 members.[15] The bulk of the recruits were Eritreans from the rural western lowlands of Barka, although young students and workers from the highlands and from urban centers in the Sudan and Egypt had also begun to join.

From the very beginning the problem with the ELF was its lack of a clear political line and a disciplined organization. This was to prove critical in the split that occurred later. As Osman Saleh Sabbe, a leading member during this period, has since written, "The leadership of the front—myself one of them—committed a serious mistake by giving priority to the gun instead of the organization."[16]

Very few meetings were held and in the few that there were, there was no participation of the rank and file. The meetings were not conducted in a democratic spirit: instead the leadership imposed its ideas—feudal style. Idris Mohammed Adam became a princely figure and his entourage of incompetent sycophants a princely constellation. All of them resided abroad. Competence and dedication were often penalized in favor of parochial loyalty and ignorance. Demands for change, made in the name of effectively prosecuting the armed struggle, were denied and often resulted in imprisonment, banishment, or death for the petitioner.

This organizational style and lack of clear political line affected the guerrilla army in the field. The lack of ideological unity and clear program was later exacerbated when at a meeting in Kassala in 1965 the field was divided into five military areas (like the Algerian *willaya*), along ethnic, regional, and religious lines, each with a commander who was virtually autonomous. Each regional commander soon became a "warlord" with the power of life and death, and there was intense rivalry among the regions, which even led to one regional command failing to help another that was under enemy attack. The Ethiopian government, fully aware of these conditions, was able to take advantage of them when it launched its 1967 military offensive, which began the massive devastation and exodus of civilian refugees to the Sudan that has since become the hallmark of the armed conflict in Eritrea.

As increasing numbers of politically conscious youth—mostly urban workers, students, and teachers—joined the struggle, the ELF leadership became increasingly repressive, and the opposition increasingly united. Finally, in September 1968, three of the five regional commanders were united under a slogan of democracy and unity, and a meeting was called in Adobha. The ELF leadership, which controlled the other two commands, initially tried to resist the pressure from the rank and file, but finally agreed to attend. The meeting called for the establishment of a *provisional* general command, to replace the old command based abroad, and to unify the regional commands. It was to last a year, after which a congress was to be convened. A preparatory committee and a commission of inquiry into past crimes were also established.

The ELF leadership, which still controlled arms and had a large following, had only agreed to gain time, however, and they proceeded to assassinate some of the leading members of the opposition, banish others, and bribe still others into silence with the perquisites of "office." They did not learn from, let alone bow to, the wishes of the masses, as represented by the tripartite agreement of the Adobha meeting. Adobha became a synonym for intrigue and betrayal and all hopes for working within the ELF for a democratic national liberation struggle were dashed. The stage was set for the emergence of the Eritrean People's Liberation Front.

## The Eritrean People's Liberation Front
## and the Civil War, 1970–1974

Some of those who had been agitating for a unified armed struggle, and for convening the congress at Adobha, survived the subsequent betrayal and regrouped. One group had escaped to the mountain area furthest from the ELF-dominated areas, the Ala hills, in the southern highlands. In an expression of solidarity with the Cuban struggle, Ala was renamed Sierra Maestra. A second group survived within ELF-held areas in the northwest; and a third included those who had escaped into the Sudan, flown across to Aden, and opened a new front in the Afar region of southeastern Eritrea. The EPLF emerged in April 1970, when the first and third groups split from the ELF and then cooperated in their defense against ELF attacks; the merger was formalized in September 1973. The remaining group joined them in June 1974.

Immediately after the initial split, the EPLF issued a clearly articulated political program entitled "Our Struggle and Its Goals," which was distributed inside Eritrea as well as abroad. The immediate response of the general command of the ELF, which felt its interests threatened, was to launch a military attack. This was opposed by the mass of ELF fighters at various meetings in the field, and the general command was forced to back off. A faction of the general command residing abroad resurrected the idea of a congress, hoping to obtain legitimacy and an excuse for the attack. A preparatory committee was assembled hastily, and a commission of inquiry similarly revived, but only to investigate administrative and political defects and to recommend remedies.

The congress was held in the Sudan in December 1971, under the auspices of the general command, now renamed the Revolutionary Council (hereafter referred to as ELF-RC). Three months later, armed with the congress's approval, and with the help of recently recruited educated Eritreans, the ELF-RC declared war on the EPLF. It thus chose to forget the real enemy and instead turn against another national organization. It produced a "political program" that was only an additional smokescreen for its military activities, and whose words were belied by these actions.

As the civil war progressed, increasing numbers of politically conscious people within the ELF and from among the Eritrean population began to exert pressure for it to be brought to a halt. The EPLF, for its part, adopted a defensive posture and refused to attack, but at the same time proved to be militarily and politically a formidable opponent. Finally, in January 1975, after nearly three years of heavy sacrifice, the civil war came to an end.

The report of the ceasefire was not well received by the Dergue. As noted earlier, the crushing defeat of Haile Selassie's forces at the hands of the EPLF in January 1974 had precipitated the crisis that allowed the Dergue to come to power. Later, in November 1974, the first head of the Dergue had made a serious effort to bring about a negotiated settlement. After his death, the Dergue embarked upon a wave of atrocities in Eritrea, and this, along with the ceasefire, led to a mass exodus of young Eritreans from Ethiopia to join both the guerrilla fronts in more or less equal numbers.[17] The Dergue panicked, and on February 1, 1975, launched an offensive around Asmara. This ended in humiliating defeat in battles near Adi Nifas and Beleza, during which the EPLF displayed superior discipline and fighting ability and gained the whole-hearted support of the Eritrean people. The armed struggle, which had hitherto been confined to the low-lands and to the northern and southern mountains, now reached the gates of Asmara and reverberated throughout the country, involving the entire population.

## The EPLF and the Issue of the United Front

The EPLF's program called for a national democratic revolution. It was nationalist in its belief that national liberation demands national unity, and that this in turn demands that narrowly based ethnic, religious, and regional divisions be overcome and an Eritrean nation be created in which every national group is equal. It was revolutionary in that its aims went beyond the limited goal of national independence to the consummation of a national democratic revolution and the establishment of a society free from all exploitation. And it was democratic in that its aim was to establish a society in which there would be no privilege based on class or anything else, but rather full participation by everyone on an equal basis.

Although these aims had formed the basis of EPLF political and social programs since its establishment, they were given open approval at the first congress in January 1977. The resolutions passed at the congress served as guidelines for the continuing revolutionary struggle. They called upon the Eritrean people to be prepared for a long and arduous struggle, to persist in their efforts to obtain a principled unity and to overcome the difficulties caused by internal and external enemies.[18] They reaffirmed the EPLF's military strategy of liberating the land step by step, and to that end resolved "to give priority to putting greater efforts into the organization, politicization, and arming of the masses," by expanding and consolidating the mass organization of workers, peasants, women, youth, and students and arming the most conscious members of the mass organizations.

The congress also expressed solidarity with revolutionary and anti-imperialist struggles in the region and throughout the world, and stressed the importance of building close relations with other liberation movements, revolutionary organizations, and socialist countries. Self-reliance was primary, but international support and solidarity were also important.

Ever since the ceasefire, the question of uniting the fronts had been raised. The EPLF held that there should be a united front, with common services, programs, and a combined high command. When a common level of awareness, and thus ideological unity, was achieved, there would be also principled unity. The ELF, on the other hand, argued that there should be complete unity at all levels immediately.

These different approaches to national unity stem from a basic difference as to the nature and aim of the armed struggle. The ELF held that the first task was to achieve a military victory over the occupying army, and that revolutionary change would come after independence. The EPLF, on the other hand, held that the strategy for national independence was a protracted people's war, which would involve the revolutionary transformation of the feudal-bourgeois society and would be achieved through self-reliance. Outside aid was secondary, and even potentially crippling, leading to dependence on outside powers. In line with this difference, the EPLF placed its reliance primarily on the Eritrean masses, whereas the ELF gave priority to outside help (from certain Arab countries), with self-reliance coming second. Thus, despite the improved language of its program, the ELF has failed to translate this into action. The reverse has been the case for the EPLF, which has grown in size, while the ELF has shrunk.

The two organizations not only had to come to terms with each other, but each had developed internal divisions that hampered the development of an alliance. The EPLF's foreign mission in Beirut was headed by Osman Saleh Sabbe, who had once been an ELF supporter but who had agreed to a tactical alliance with the EPLF at the time when it was encircled by the ELF. The EPLF needed arms and other supplies, which Sabbe, who had over the years developed close ties with some Arab governments, had access to; Sabbe, for his part, needed a legitimate armed struggle to justify his continued request for financial assistance.

Despite this apparent coincidence of aims, Sabbe's conception of the Eritrean revolution was a far cry from that of the EPLF. It did not include a national democratic revolution, principally because Sabbe saw himself as the sole legitimate leader of the struggle and sought to dictate its aims and directions—which was of course rejected by the EPLF. Sabbe's diplomatic skills and other leadership qualities, as well as his earlier services to the Eritrean struggle, were beyond dispute, but the struggle had overtaken him, as he realized when he visited the field in April 1975. It was at this point that he decided to seek "unity" with the ELF. He realized that the EPLF line was different from his own, and he was determined that an immediate merger with the more conservative ELF would be to his advantage. So, without the knowledge of the EPLF leadership in the field, he met with Abdallah Idris, the head of the military bureau of the ELF-RC, in Baghdad in July, under the auspices of the Iraqui Baathist government. This meeting was immediately followed by another in Beirut, where the entire EPLF foreign mission, led by Sabbe, met with members of the ELF-RC central committee in Abdallah's presence. It was there decided to hold a formal meeting of the ELF and EPLF leadership in Khartoum in September.

In Khartoum, only Sabbe and the rest of the foreign mission, which he dominated, met with an enlarged leadership committee which represented the ELF-RC. When the meeting's call for a unification congress was later rejected by the EPLF, at a meeting in Semenawi Bahri in Eritrea in the fall of 1975, Sabbe was furious and began to use his Arab contacts to apply an "embargo" type of pressure on the EPLF, by freezing all aid in the pipeline. He then called a meeting in March 1976, which the EPLF leadership attended and which resulted in a complete rupture between the two. Sabbe then announced the formation of a "third front," the Eritrean Liberation Front–Popular Liberation Forces (ELF/PLF), and took with him all the aid that had been given to the EPLF in the name of the Eritrean people.

Whereas the EPLF totally rejected Sabbe's front, the ELF was divided. The ELF-RC, headed by Abdallah Idris, favored recognition or even a merger hoping to take advantage of Sabbe's access to vast amounts of money and weaponry, as well as to the oil-rich Arab leaders. When Sabbe realized that his elitist conception of the Eritrean struggle was rejected by the EPLF, he resorted to divisive tactics, appealing to Muslim religious fanaticism. This may have appealed to some of the ELF leadership, but was rejected by the rank and file of the EPLF, and to a large extent by the ELF as well. A fraction of the ELF leadership, along with the majority of its fighters, therefore rejected Sabbe's new front. These differences plunged the ELF into crisis, with recriminations, arrests, and mass desertions, all of which further reduced the size of the ELF guerrilla army. One speculation was that Sabbe encouraged these internal divisions, apparently hoping to bring about the collapse of the ELF and thus be able to focus on an EPLF that he expected to be weakened by the strain of fighting alone against the Ethiopian army. Sabbe's front could then emerge as the sole representative of the Muslim-dominated lowlands, and could demand a Lebanon-style division of Eritrea, failing a solution in which he would be the dominant figure. It is ironic that Sabbe should have sought the demise of the ELF-RC since it had facilitated the entry of his forces into western Eritrea over the objections of both the EPLF and many rank-and-file ELF members. Up until late October 1977, the ELF-RC had demanded his inclusion in unity talks in order to gain an ally against the stronger EPLF. When the rank and file had objected, the ELF-RC had reversed its position and decided to hold unity talks without the Sabbe group. This time some of its more right-wing members defected to join the Sabbe group.

On October 20, 1977, the EPLF and ELF met and made considerable progress toward unity. The meeting agreed on full independence for Eritrea as a common goal, on opposition to all forces that intervened to deny that goal, on safeguards for the democratic rights of the Eritrean masses, and on the establishment of good relations with all progressive forces in the world. At a further meeting in April 1978, they agreed to implement the earlier agreement by laying out a program for coordinating military, economic, foreign, political, and propaganda affairs.

The Dergue decided to counter these unity efforts before they became concrete, this time with Soviet backing. In November 1978, it launched an offensive which resulted in the recapture of all ELF-held towns and some held by the EPLF, and finally in the securing of the strategic city of Keren. The unity efforts may thus have been too late and too little. Although the two fronts met again in January 1979 and subsequently, and reaffirmed the April accord, one can only hope that the bitter lesson of the previous years has not been in vain.

The issue of unity is of grave concern to all Eritreans. For it is possible that if the Eritrean forces had been united, the Ethiopian army, which in 1977 was limited to the capital and two isolated cities, would have surrendered. Mengistu's survival depends on his success in crushing the "rebels" in Eritrea, as he has vowed to do ever since his emergence as the effective leader of the Dergue. It is only with Russian help, and Eritrean disunity, that he has so far been able to maintain his regime.

## The Supreme Test of the Revolution

The armed struggle in Eritrea is the longest in African history, and one of the longest in the world. It has been a bitter and costly struggle, with many twists and turns. It has also transformed Eritrean society and, led by the EPLF, has instituted impressive social and economic programs and political organization, which have gained it the loyalty and support of the peasant and urban masses, including students, teachers, and intellectuals. Only this success can explain its exraordinary survival in the face of the Dergue's massive and Soviet-backed military offensive, which began in early July 1978. It is unnecessary to list the enormous costs, human and material, that the Dergue has sustained since that time; suffice it to say that a small nation, properly organized and fighting for the survival of its revolution, has defeated a numerically much superior aggressor army.

The Dergue committed two-thirds of its entire armed forces (regular and militia) to Eritrea in order to crush the Eritreans in two or three months. The first offensive failed, and was followed by a second, launched on December 18, 1978. Over 120,000 troops were deployed, advised, and organized by high-ranking Soviet officers, with Soviet logistical support, heavy armory, weapons, and air power.[19] Faced with this, the EPLF decided on a strategy of withdrawal to their bases in Sahel; this meant abandoning positions won in 1977 and early 1978, including the city of Keren and other strategic towns and villages, and interrupting the process of social transformation.[20] The strategy paid off, however. Three more large-scale offensives followed, with the final one in the Sahel region in July 1979 ending in defeat for the Dergue. The Ethiopian army then became bogged down in Sahel, and the EPLF was able to begin its own offensive in early December 1979, overrunning Ethiopian bases and dislodging the Ethiopian army from several strategic positions.[21]

Impressive as this military success is, of equally far-reaching significance is the degree of self-reliance found in the mountains and valleys of Sahel. This has been possible not only because the EPLF has at its command a well-trained, experienced, and heroic guerrilla army with a well-organized supply system, and has not had to abandon positions and roam far afield in search of food, as the ELF army often had to do. More important, the EPLF's political program and its faithful translation of this into practice has enabled it to build a strong organization, and to continue to generate new cadres. This in turn has made it possible to expand and intensify the mobilization and politicization of the peasantry, workers, and others in the working population. Women, youth, and other groupings in the towns and villages have participated in popular elections, choosing representatives to mass organizations. A militia, including both men and women, has been organized, as have literacy campaigns and schools, medical and other social services, all of which reach remote villages that have never before known such services. People's stores and cooperative shops have been organized to meet the basic needs at local market prices, eliminating the middleman's exploitative "mark-up." The cooperatives provide the bulk of the army's food and other needs, while the workshops repair vehicles, weapons, radios, watches, and other equipment. There is sophisticated carpentry and textile work. Skills are being passed on to the younger fighters, paving the way for a future industrial workforce. In a word, since 1975 the EPLF has been running and building a state.

It is time the progressive world paid serious attention to this David and Goliath spectacle, now beginning its third year, and react appropriately to a war in which a so-called socialist power has committed men, weapons, and its prestige to defeat the cause of freedom and revolution which it once supported as just.

# 4

## The Oromo and the Tigray: National Liberation and Crisis of Empire

The issues pertaining to the national question in the context of the Ethiopian empire were outlined in the introductory chapter, together with the various forces involved in the struggle. Here the national question will be discussed in some detail by reference to two main national liberation struggles in the Horn— among the Oromo and the Tigray peoples. The struggle over the Ogaden will be dealt with in the next chapter. In all of these cases, and that of Eritrea, there is a common enemy, and for that reason, among others, all are interested in the liquidation and transformation of the Ethiopian empire. The central underlying issue is the right to self-determination, which the Ethiopian government has sought to deny by manipulating the Leninist principle. The inheritors of the Ethiopian feudo-imperial state, surveying the oppressed nations from the dizzy heights of their newly acquired power, have dismissed their national aspirations as "unpatriotic," "un-Ethiopian," the "weapon of reaction" or "imperialism," and have made repeated references to Lenin in support of their position. It is therefore appropriate to review Lenin's discussion of this question.

### The Leninist Principle of Self-Determination

To begin with, what is a nation? A standard definition is that it is a "historically evolved, stable community of language, territory, economic life, and psychological make-up manifested in a community of culture"[1]—a definition that would easily encompass all the nations within the Ethiopian state. Lenin believed that an "oppressed nation"—one denied the right to exercise any of these components—had the right to self-determination, *up to and including secession.* This did not mean, however, that secession could be undertaken at any time on any slightest pretext, for achieving self-determination was related to the goal of achieving socialism:

> The aim of socialism is not only to end the division of mankind into tiny states and the isolation of nations in any form, it is not only to bring the nations closer together but to integrate them. . . . In the same way as mankind can arrive at the abolition of classes only through a transition period of the dictatorship of the oppressed class, it can arrive at the inevitable integration of nations only through a transition period of the complete emancipation of all oppressed nations, i.e., their freedom to secede.[2]

Those who, in the name of Leninism, seek to deny nations the right to self-determination are doing violence both to theory and to the nations themselves:

> Socialist parties which did not show by all their activity, both now, during the revolution, and after its victory, that they would liberate the enslaved nations and build up relations with them on the basis of a free union—and free union is a false phrase without the right to secede—these parties would be betraying socialism.[3]

Nor should a victorious socialism rest until full democracy is established, and "consequently, not only introduce full equality of nations but also realise the right of the oppressed nations to self-determination, i.e., the right to free political separation."[4]

The Ethiopian military regime and its foreign allies, however, speak not of the oppressed peoples' need for national self-determination, but of the need for an inter-nation (or supra-nation) class solidarity—a solidarity of the working classes of the oppressed and oppressor nations. Lenin had a response to this tactic as well:

> The proletariat of the oppressor nations must not confine themselves to general stereotyped phrase against annexation and in favor of the equality of nations in general, such as any

pacifist bourgeois will repeat. The proletariat cannot remain silent on the question of the *frontiers* of a state founded on national oppression. . . The proletariat must struggle against the enforced retention of oppressed nations within the bounds of the given state, which means that they must fight for the right to self-determination. The proletariat must demand freedom of political separation for the colonies and nations oppressed by "their own" nations. *Otherwise, the internationalism of the proletariat would be nothing but empty words; neither confidence nor class solidarity would be possible between the workers of the oppressed and oppressor nations.*[5] (Emphasis added.)

The national liberation groups, whose resistance predated the Ethiopian revolution by many years, hoped that it would meet their aspirations, and many joined hands with Ethiopian revolutionaries in a spirit of solidarity. When the revolution failed them, they took to the hills and planned a protracted people's war, based in the rural areas. The Oromo Liberation Front (OLF) and the Tigray People's Liberation Front (TPLF) have espoused Marxism-Leninism, but their ultimate goals are somewhat different. The TPLF emphasizes the need for a social revolution in Ethiopia, but reserves the right to secede if need be. Its ultimate goal is not as clear-cut and singleminded as that of the OLF, which aims at establishing the People's Republic of Oromia; and although the Oromo might wish to share in a democratic Ethiopian revolution, they are for now calling themselves separatist. The Western Somalia (Ogaden) Liberation Front (WSLF), which will be discussed more fully in the next chapter, is somewhat different in that it is divided into two wings, the stronger of which does not openly espouse Marxism-Leninism and wants not only secession but union with Somalia. Some of its territorial claims are the same as those of the OLF, however, which brings them into direct conflict. Thus although the TPLF and the Eritrean struggles in the north reinforce each other, the division between the OLF and the WSLF in the south has weakened their ability to fight a common enemy.

The Eritrean struggle is distinguished from all these in that it is a colonial, not a national, question, as defined by the prevailing international legal order. This makes Eritrea unique in the region, but it does not, and should not, make the right to self-determination of the Oromos, the Tigreans, and the Somalis of the Ogaden any less valid. The United Nations Charter, and subsequent resolutions (e.g., Resolution 2625 [xxv]) clearly give nations and peoples this right to self-determination.

## The Oromo

The history of the Oromo and of their advent into what is today southern, western, and eastern Ethiopia has been a subject of great debate. Oromo oral tradition traces their homeland to an area called Hora Walaabu, in the southern part of present-day Ethiopia, between Lake Rudolph and Lake Abaya. Although several historical accounts treat the Oromo people as alien to this region, recent studies by anthropologists, historians, and linguists have produced evidence that confirms the tradition.[6] Further, the earliest documents on the subject, written by the Abyssinian monk Abba Bahrey in 1593, state that the Oromo people "crossed the river of their country which is called Galana to the frontier of Bale in the time of Atse Wanag Sagad [1508–1540]"[7] and the Galana is in the Hora Walaabu.

The Oromo are roughly divided into five major groupings, which are sometimes called tribes, but are in fact clans: people who believe that they are descended from a common ancestor, and who speak a mutually intelligible language and share a common culture. The five clans are Mecha, Tulema, Borana, Bartumma, and Wallo, and are linked historically through five "fathers" who were the first war leaders and who established themselves in different regions, where they remain to this day. They are primarily in the southern, eastern, western, and central provinces of the Ethiopian empire, with a few in the north (in Wallo and Raya Azabo in the southern Tigray provinces).

Population estimates for the Oromo range from a conservative figure of 15 million (which would be over 50 percent of the population of the entire empire) to 18 million.[8] Even using the most conservative figure, the Oromo—next to the Fulani and

the Hausa—form the largest grouping in sub-Saharan Africa that speaks a mutually intelligible language. The Oromo engage in pastoralism and mixed herding and agriculture in widely differing geographical areas, ranging from the desert plain of eastern Shoa and Hararghe to the rich farmland of the southern and western regions.

The Oromo people came into peripheral contact with the Abyssinian kingdom during the Gondarine dynasty in the early eighteenth century, but a more decisive relationship—one consummated by conquest—did not come until Menelik began his expansion to the south in the late nineteenth century. The Oromo national movement, which surfaced in the urban centers in the mid-1960s, had its roots in the resistance of the 1880s and 1890s. Menelik's policy of conquest and "pacification" sought the

alliance of certain Oromo leaders, who received material inducements and positions in the feudal bureaucracy. In their turn,
they gave up their language and culture for the Amharic language
and culture, and took part in attempts to make the rest of the
population do the same. Many of the collaborators rose to the
highest ranks of the feudal aristocracy. The most famous of these
was Ras Gobena, whose case exemplifies the clash of two cultures
and the inducements offered by the perquisites of office of the
conquering nation. Gobena was a leading Oromo official, elected
for a term of eight years under the *gada* system. Knowing that he
could not be reelected, Gobena made his "expert" services
available to Menelik; he was amply rewarded with large *gult*
rights—the *gult* system being alien to Oromo culture. As with
most subsequent Oromo converts, Gobena also converted from
his traditional beliefs to the Ethiopian Orthodox Christian religion. The effects this had on increasing social status made a
quick conversion desirable and encouraged excessive zeal. For
one thing, a convert was permitted to sit near the king or his
representative at a banquet, and presence at such a banquet
(called the *gibr*) was the most dramatic proof of high status.

Such insidious processes undermined Oromo cohesion, and
affected their culture in many ways. Christian converts had
churches built on the sites of local shrines or places of worship, a
method of undermining the foundations of Oromo culture that
was aided by European missionaries. For instance, one of these,
a German named Ludwig Krapf, felt that the Oromo "would, if
only they accepted Christ, lead [read: dominate] their less for-
tunate and less numerous neighbors militarily, economically,
spiritually, and culturally."[9] At the same time, the use of the
Oromo language was systematically forbidden. Even preaching
in Oromo in church was prohibited. As P. T. W. Baxter reported
in 1967:

> I sat through a mission church [in Arusi] at which the preacher
> and all the congregation were Oromo but at which the sermon, as
> well as the service, was given in Amharinya [Amharic], which few
> of the congregation understood at all, and then translated into
> Oromo. The farce had to be played out in case a Judas informed
> and the district officer fined or imprisoned the preacher.[10]

In addition, Oromo schoolchildren, like all schoolchildren in Ethiopia, had to go through primary school in Amharic, and every child who sought higher education had to pass an examination in Amharic, even though higher education was in English. The effect of this legislation was not only to exclude millions of Oromo children from higher education, but to unite the Oromo in their sense of deprivation, with language standing at the heart of it. Further, Oromo as a language fell behind, while Amharic developed dramatically in the 1960s and early 1970s in Ethiopia, particularly in terms of its political vocabulary. The prohibition of the use of Oromo thus denied that language (as well as the languages of other oppressed nations) the opportunity for a similar development.

Such policies, however, often provoked the response that had been feared. For instance, during the Italian occupation, masses of Arsi Oromo from highland Arusi province accepted Islam, in a large measure as a demonstration of anti-Amhara sentiment and a rejection of all values associated with the imperial conquerors. This was part of the first stage of the Oromo people's resistance movement. This stage consisted of spontaneous expressions of resistance to oppression and expropriation in the aftermath of Menelik's conquest, and included a series of rebellions by the Raya and Azebo (on the northern fringe of the Oromo nation) between 1928 and 1930. This first stage ended with the consolidation of the Ethiopian state under Haile Selassie. The history of this period, which has hitherto been told in the hushed voices of the underground, is only beginning to be pieced together, primarily from oral histories. Learning of the heroic deeds of the Oromo people and their leaders in this period will be an important aspect of their liberation.

The second stage of the Oromo national liberation struggle began with the organization of the Mecha-Tulema movement in 1965. (Mecha and Tulema were two of the pioneering founders of the Oromo nation.) It was organized by the newly created Oromo petty bourgeoisie, and attempted to involve the Oromo masses in the cities and the countryside, especially in Arusi. It was led by Tadesse Birru, who had been a general in the Ethiopian police force and then in the territorial army; he was an "assimilated" Oromo from the central province of Shoa, and a devout Christian. During the attempted coup in 1960, he had been a leader of the powerful police commando brigade in Addis Ababa, and had thrown his lot with the loyalists. He was rewarded with an appointment as deputy head of the emperor's militia (known as the territorial army). Because of his past loyalty, and also because he had an Amharic name, Prime Minister Aklilu Habte Wold took him for an Amhara and told him in private that in the recruitment and promotion of soldiers, care should be taken to restrict the number of Oromo. This incident shocked Tadesse out of his blind devotion to the emperor, and soon thereafter he began to help organize the Mecha-Tulema movement—much to the chagrin of Aklilu and other Amhara leaders. A bomb explosion in an Addis Ababa cinema in 1966 was attributed to him and to Mamo Mezemir, a young Oromo graduate of the Harar Military Academy. When Tadesse and other leaders were arrested and the movement banned in 1967, its members went underground. The younger and more militant began to organize among Oromo peasants and urban dwellers, using the organizational infrastructure established by the Mecha-Tulema movement, and laying the groundwork for the Oromo Liberation Front.

The Oromo, like other Ethiopians, welcomed the revolution of 1974 with great expectations, particularly with the announcement of the Dergue's rural land reform program, which promised to benefit the conquered peoples of southern Ethiopia, the bulk of whom were Oromo. No sooner had these measures been taken, however, than the Oromo made further demands for self-determination, encompassing other spheres of their life. For instance, the farmers' associations, formed to take the place of the old feudal structures in the rural areas, were conceived of very differently by the Dergue and the Oromo, who wanted to elect their own representatives freely. The Oromo started to make political demands which particularly focused on the total denial of their right to use their own language—remembering that the Oromo compose the largest single nation within Ethiopia. This single demographic fact has sharpened Oromo national consciousness and provided fuel for the pan-Oromo political activity organized by the OLF.

The Dergue's response to these demands was a mixture of anger, puzzlement, and perfidy. Its nine-point program, which promised autonomy to all regions, also promised token broadcasting programs in the Oromo language. Baxter notes the extent to which "educated Oromos bitterly resent being deprived of the use of their native language for anything but domestic purposes, and particularly when it is the first language of a nation of some ten million or so people."[11] The OLF organized protests and further demands, including that the Oromo language be used in more broadcasting, that there be an Oromo-language daily newspaper, that Oromo be used in teaching elementary school students, in preaching, and for official government business. The Dergue's response was predictably negative.

## The OLF Leadership and Its Program

The leadership of the OLF included primarily the young, educated children of the urban petty bourgeoisie, small traders, bureaucrats, and tenant farmers. Most came from the province of Wallaga, which had had early exposure to European missionary education, and which had been spared the spoilation and humiliation suffered by Oromo in other provinces at the hand of Menelik's army because Kumsa, one of their leaders, had offered Menelik the gold of Wallaga in return for protection. Menelik then made Kumsa chief of most of the people of Wallaga, with all the rights and privileges of that office.

The Wallaga Oromo were thus able to develop in a relatively peaceful atmosphere, and this, along with mission education, made them the intellectual leaders of the Oromo nation. Ridiculed in their fight to master Amharic, they were keenly aware of the galvanizing power of the language question. But although significant progress has been made in reinstating Oromo, Amharic is still the official medium of instruction and communication, which has hampered the Oromo. There are a few Oromo journals, however, including *Qaanqee*, which was started by Oromo university students in 1974 and was in both English and Amharic, *Sagalee Bosona*, the official organ of the military wing of the

OLF, and several journals in Ethiopia and the United States.

The OLF announced its program in October 1974 in Finfine (the old Oromo name for Addis Ababa), and amended it in June 1976.[12] After outlining the history of the Oromo people—their conquest by Menelik's army, their subjugation, and their early resistance—the program analyzed the recent struggle of the Oromo nation. It raised the question of who were friends and who were enemies in the struggle and answered in no uncertain terms: the enemies included the Ethiopian colonial regime, the Oromo feudal class, the neo-Gobanists—a name coined after Ras Gobena to describe traitors to the Oromo cause—and international imperialism. The friends included the Ethiopian working class, which is "viciously exploited by the alliance of state capitalism and imperialism," regardless of its place of origin or work, and the peasantry, "one of the leading stars of the usurped February [1974] democratic revolution." The program bitterly attacked the regime's denial of the peasants' demand to arm themselves.

Other supporters of the struggle were the petty bourgeoisie, patriotic elements, the revolutionary intelligentsia, members of the armed forces, and other oppressed nations: the petty bourgeoisie included small merchants, craftsmen, teachers, students, and lower-level government employees; the intelligentsia was defined as "those who often are willing to forego the complacency of their daily lives in favor of the liberation of their people"; and the armed forces contained large numbers of Oromo who were conscious of their oppressed status, and who would, if an organization devoted to the liberation of their fellow nationals existed, join the ranks of the revolution.

The overall objective of the struggle, according to the program, was "the realization of national self-determination for the Oromo people and their liberation from oppression and exploitation in all their forms." This could only be realized through "the successful consummation of the new democratic revolution by waging an anti-feudal, anti-colonial, and anti-imperialist struggle, and by the establishment of a people's democratic republic of Oromia." Specific goals included vesting power in a people's congress, instituting free and democratic rights for all anti-feudal, anti-colonial, and anti-imperialist classes, establishing a secular government that would respect the quality of all religions and beliefs, and establishing a democratic legal system that would promote, protect, and guarantee basic and fundamental human rights. To this was added a list of economic, educational, and social objectives, including the organization of the peasant masses in a manner that would consolidate the "revolutionary gain of the people with regard to agrarian reform." To that end, the program proposed assistance to pastoralists that would settle them and educate them "to realize all their capabilities," the nationalization of all unoccupied land with a view to establishing state farms, and the nationalization "of all national resources, financial institutions, transport and communication media, and all industries and enterprises vital to the national economy and defense." The program, referring to the settlement of Amhara from central Shoa, opposed the "massive resettlement program in Oromia by others while the Oromo people are suffocating due to lack of sufficient land."

Education, health, welfare, labor, and women were all treated under different headings, and proposals included the provision of free education and health programs, the guarantee of work for all, the institution of social security for the unemployed and handicapped, full equality for women, paid maternity leave, and the creation of a women's organization to safeguard women's rights. In the field of culture the program envisaged the elimination of the "reactionary feudal, colonial, imperialist culture," and its replacement by the "national, scientific mass culture of the new democracy on the basis of popular elements in Oromo culture." Art, literature, and music were to be encouraged, and the Oromo language (using the Latin alphabet) was to be developed to "bring it out of the neglect that colonialism has imposed upon it."

The program then called for the establishment of a people's militia "committed to the defense of the nation," and a people's revolutionary army that would participate in development projects.

The OLF program has drawn a considerable number of the intelligentsia and some members of the petty bourgeoisie into the organization's ranks, but it remains to be seen how successful it will be with the peasantry, and that in turn will depend on how well the OLF is able to translate the principles contained in the program into daily practice.[13]

## The OLF Struggle

The OLF quickly gained widespread support from groups of Oromo students, within Ethiopia, in Europe, and in the United States, each of which published a journal. The student organizations have not only been the principal points of contact between the OLF and the outside world, but they have also played a crucial role in articulating the objectives, problems, and prospects of the struggle, and are an important source of recruitment and political training for OLF cadres. They are receiving increased attention from Oromo in Ethiopia itself: for instance, the annual congress of Oromo in the United States in August 1979 was attended by an OLF representative from the field, an event which had a catalytic effect on the organization's membership, which has since doubled. That these ties have been so late in coming is in part due to distance and other logistical problems, but must also be viewed in the light of the Ethiopian regime's repressive security network, which has meant that care has had to be taken to first build an organizational base within Ethiopia.

While waging armed struggle and steadily gaining strength in the countryside, the OLF has intensified its political struggle as well. It now reaches most of Oromo areas through its three organs, *Bakkalcha Oromo,* the organ of the OLF as a whole, *Warraqa,* the organ of its youth wing, and *Sagalee Bosona,* the organ serving the eastern branch of the OLF army. It also struggles with the Dergue directly on cultural and linguistic issues: for instance, when urban groups demanded that they be able to use their language for teaching at least grades 1 to 6, the Dergue's rejection of this demand led to protest demonstrations in Harar and Jimma in September 1978, which were suppressed violently, with some 250 students killed. The military government has temporarily "finessed" the OLF's attempt to create a people's militia and a people's development army by using the threat of outside invasion to convince Oromo that it is more important to join the Ethiopian army. But as a result arms have been distributed to large numbers of peasants, including Oromo.

## The Contradictions of the Struggle

The Oromo movement in general, and the OLF in particular, has come into conflict with other movements in the region. Not only has the position of the Ethiopian left on the national question been noncommital at best, but, far more serious, the Western Somalia Liberation Front (and the Somali government) has laid claim to Oromo areas that they regard as "lost" Somali territory. The OLF, on the other hand, has made a number of allegations against the Somali government and the WSLF: that Oromo exiled in Somalia have been mistreated, that the Somali government has failed to support the OLF, that the WSLF has even carried out sabotage in such Oromo areas as Dire Dawa, Jijiga, Haremaia, Ginir, Negelle, and that the WSLF has at the same time claimed credit for some OLF operations.[14] Further, Somali policies were creating divisions among the Oromo on religious and national lines, while the idea of a Greater Somalia has been used by the Ethiopian government as an excuse to commit atrocities against Oromo, Adere, and Somali in the eastern part of the empire.[15]

This particular contradiction is now being resolved, as we will explain in more detail in the chapter on the WSLF. At this point it is sufficient to note that the Somali government has recognized the OLF as a legitimate national liberation front, and in late 1979 gave it permission to open an office in Mogadishu.

## Tigray

Tigray lies in the northern part of Ethiopia, bordered on the north and northeast by Eritrea, on the south and southwest by the Ethiopian provinces of Wallo and Begemdir (Gondar), and on the west by the Sudan. It has an area of about 102,000 sq. km.

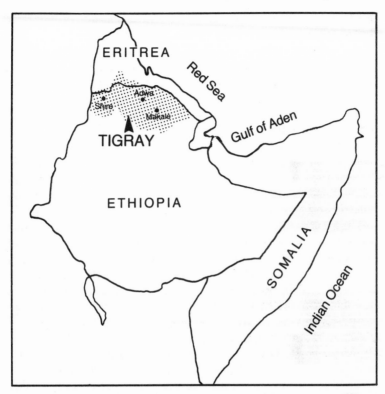

The people of Tigray are estimated to number some 5 million, including those living in the area that was added to the Wallo province after World War II. Although Afar, Saho, and other minorities live in parts of Tigray, the overwhelming majority belong to a national grouping that is descended from the Axumites and speaks Tigrinya (which is also the language of highland Eritrea).[16] Christianity and Islam are the principal religions, with Christianity adhered to by the majority.

Tigray consists of a central and southern mountainous area, with arable plateaus, a fertile lowland region to the west, and an arid and semi-arid region to the east. The elevation ranges from 128 meters below sea level in the Afar (Danakil) depression to 1500 meters in the lowlands and 2900 meters in the highlands. Agriculture is the basis of the livelihood of over 90 percent of the population, and the main crops are wheat, barley, millet, taff, maize, oats, and sorghum, as well as beans, oil-seeds, and cotton; plant products such as incense and gum arabic are exported. Halite-encrusted salt has been exploited for centuries and used as currency. Cattle, sheep, and goats are raised in great numbers. A minority of urban-dwelling Tigreans engage in trade and commerce, but there is no industry of any significance, and even the few cottage industries that exist do not function all the time. Yet Tigray is an area with deposits of potash—which has been intermittently extracted under a joint venture between an American company and the Ethiopian government—sulphur, manganese, copper, gold, zinc, lead, iron ore, and mica. Hydro-electric and geothermal power are possibilities for the future.

The resistance of the Tigrean people to Amhara rule goes back to the nineteenth century. After the chaotic period known as the "era of the princes," in the late eighteenth and early nineteenth centuries, the Gondarin rebel Kassa ascended to the Abyssinian throne under the name of Emperor Teodoros and unified a number of feuding fiefdoms; he ruled until he was forced to commit suicide following a British expedition in 1868. In 1872, a Tigrean nobleman, also named Kassa, came to the throne as Yohannes IV. Meanwhile, Menelik, a Shoan, was consolidating his kingdom and slowly expanding west and south. By the time of Yohannes' death in 1889, Menelik's expansion and empire building had engulfed the south, west, southwest, and southeast, as well as the old fiefdoms of Gojjam, Gondar, and Tigray—leaving Eritrea for the Italians.

The resistance of the people of Tigray to alien rule began at this time, while the rigor of the Shoan occupation must be seen partly in the light of the fear of a revival of Tigrean hegemony. There have been rebellions ever since. The most famous took place in 1943, and came to be known as the Woyane revolt. It destroyed Ethiopian garrisons in Tigray, defeated units of Haile Selassie's British-trained armed forces, and for a time liberated Makale, the capital. Ethiopian reinforcements were repulsed until Haile Selassie appealed for, and obtained, more British help, including airplanes to bomb Makale. The Tigrean feudal lords, led by a descendant of Yohannes named Ras Seyum, sided with the imperial government, for the revolt was popularly based and threatened their interests.

The failure of the Woyane revolt led to the disarming of the Tigrean population, the occupation of their land, and the imposition of heavy taxation. The people of Tigray have thus tasted the bitter pill of oppression and have continued to tell the growing generation about it. Those in the resistance were forced to go underground, but members of the educated and commercial classes attempted to form professional and social welfare organizations as centers for the national resistance struggle. In the early 1970s, all these efforts were united under the Tigray National Organization (TNO), which began underground political activities. During the Ethiopian revolution, the TNO played an important role in publishing and distributing agitational material and in guiding popular demonstrations. It intensified its organization of underground cells, in view of the usurpation of the fruits of the revolution by the military in September 1974, and, after having analyzed the situation in Ethiopia and in Tigray, it began to prepare for armed struggle in the countryside.[17]

Thus the latest stage of the resistance of the people of Tigray began on February 18, 1975, with the establishment of the Tigray People's Liberation Front (TPLF), which began armed struggle in the western lowlands. Its support came from the peasantry, although its leading cadres were workers, small tradesmen, teachers, and students. Its objectives were national self-determination and democratic revolution, and it proclaimed itself to be anti-imperialist, anti-Zionist, anti-feudal, anti-national oppression, and anti-fascist. Explaining its goal of national self-determination and democratic revolution, it stated:

> Self-determination does not mean secession; nor does it mean unity for the sake of unity. (a) If there is a democratic political atmosphere, it means the creation of voluntarily integrated nations and nationalities whose relations are based on equality, democracy, and mutual advantage. (b) If the existing national oppression continues or is aggravated, then it means the birth of an independent Tigray.

This statement must be viewed in the light of repeated attempts on the part of the Ethiopian government to foster divisions between Tigreans and Eritreans. Despite historic, linguistic, and cultural links that go back to the Axumite empire, attempts in the early 1940s to unite the two under the supremacy of Ras Seyum raised fears among Eritreans of being placed under a feudal Tigrean prince—a fear skillfully exploited by Haile Selassie. Such attempts in any case completely ignored Eritrean history, particularly its colonial history.

Nevertheless, the Ethiopian Democratic Union (EDU), led by Ras Menguesha (son of Ras Seyum), the last governor-general of Tigray before the revolution in 1974, made a further attempt—although from a different direction—to play on these divisions by arguing that Tigray was part of Ethiopia, and that Tigreans were Ethiopians who should fight with the EDU (whose leadership was composed of former feudal lords, high-ranking government officials, and leading members of the feudal-bourgeois class) to overthrow the Dergue, instead of waging a war of secession.

Before the TPLF had intensified its armed struggle, the EDU had attempted to win the support of the Tigrean peasantry, but its appeal was hopelessly confused: using national (Tigrean) sentiments and lamenting Amhara domination, it obtained limited support from the feudal lords and richer farmers, but its call for "greater Ethiopian unity" failed to impress the long-suffering Tigrean populace, which it in any case further taxed to support its army.

The TPLF rejected this imposition on the peasantry; instead it began a literacy campaign and to provide medical supplies and health services. Eventually it also distributed land to landless peasants. It thus rooted its struggle in the lowest stratum of the Tigrean masses, and its deeds won over the peasants in the affected districts. The EDU, for its part, waged a relentless propaganda campaign against the TPLF, and fielded an impressive army of deserters and those loyal to Ras Menguesha and other feudal lords. The stage was set for a classic confrontation between the forces of progress and those representing wealth and privilege.

Once the TPLF had begun to intensify its work in the countryside around Adwa and Makale, it was only a matter of time before the EDU forces launched an attack on them. First, attempts were made to intimidate some of the peasants, who were beginning to enjoy the early fruits of TPLF-initiated land reform. Then, in June 1976, the first armed clash occurred, followed by another in September. Both ended in TPLF victories, but the second took longer and took a heavier toll. In March 1977 some 10,000 EDU troops crossed into the Shire/Adyabo district and attacked the TPLF, which was forced to evacuate the area. It was one of TPLF's most critical moments: certain petty-bourgeois members abandoned it, a setback that the TPLF analyzed as a failure by opportunists to understand the dialectical process involved in a protracted people's war and as a purification of the front. In the end, the TPLF defeated the EDU forces, thus passing the test with flying colors, gaining immense military as well as political experience. After further heavy sacrifices in battles—at Adi Daero, Zaghir, Adi Hagheray, and Maye Khuli—and after intense political work among the peasants, the TPLF tipped the scales in its favor, and in 1978 finally chased the EDU from Tigray, pushing them beyond the Takkaze valley into Welkayit, a wilderness area south of Shire.

Throughout the TPLF's struggle against the EDU, the Dergue persisted in lumping the two together as "anti-unity" forces and "reactionary elements," along with "Eritrean secessionists" and "EPRP anarchists." When the TPLF was waging its life-and-death struggle with the EDU along clearly articulated class lines, the Dergue failed to take any stand in favor of the TPLF's united democratic front against the EDU, an anti-democratic and essentially neo-feudal force.

As a result of its success, the TPLF captured large quantities of arms and ammunition from the EDU and the Dergue, and, most important, won the support of the Tigrean peasants, who were freed from EDU levies and who became among the most ardent supporters of the TPLF. One of the political results of the hard-won victory was that the mass of the Tigrean people came to recognize the up-and-down nature of a protracted people's war, and thus maintained their support of the TPLF—by providing vital material and intelligence support—when it joined the EPLF in the summer of 1978 and scored a victory over the Dergue's army. When the Dergue launched its counteroffensive against Eritrea from Tigray, hoping to eliminate the TPLF on the way, it failed miserably in its later objective. The TPLF, far from being eliminated, gained arms and equipment when it made a series of bold attacks on Dergue garrisons in the Tembien district of Tigray.

The TPLF victory also had significant results in the foreign diplomatic sphere. Some neighboring countries acknowledged their mistake in underestimating the TPLF and giving unqualified support to the EDU and now recognized the TPLF as the legitimate representative of the Tigrean people. Among other things, this made it possible for the TPLF to organize Tigrean refugees openly into mass support organizations.

The TPLF faced a second obstacle, besides the EDU. This was the EPRA, the EPRP army stationed in Tigray, some of whose more prominent leaders were Tigrean. While the EPRP and the TPLF both used the language of liberation of the oppressed masses, and although their programs appeared at first to be indistinguishable, they differed on the issue of whether nations, and nationalities, had the right to struggle against their own national oppression separately from—although in cooperation with—a multinational revolutionary struggle waged by a group such as EPRP. This raised the vexing question of the ultimate objective of a national struggle such as that being waged by the TPLF, and led not only to long debates but in the end to armed clashes between two groups that had far more to gain from cooperation. As the program quoted above indicates, the TPLF was not calling for the immediate establishment of an independent people's republic of Tigray; its struggle was not posed as an anti-colonial struggle, but as a national liberation struggle. The TPLF stand contrasts with that of the OLF in this respect—indeed, there are Tigreans who call for the establishment of a people's republic of Tigray irrespective of the nature of the government in Addis Ababa. The EPRP, on the other hand, argued that class consciousness should transcend or absorb any national consciousness, and thus that all national struggles should be subordinated to the multinational struggle being waged by the EPRP. It thus argued that Tigray was an integral part of Ethiopia, and that the EPRP, as an all-Ethiopian organization, was the only legitimate body to conduct a liberation campaign in Tigray. Its choice of Tigray as a base was due to its proximity to Eritrea, a source of support and refuge.

On the Eritrean question, the TPLF argued that this was an anti-colonial struggle, while the EPRP regarded it as a national question in the context of "greater Ethiopia." Here too the TPLF position differed from that of the OLF, which failed to call the Eritrean struggle a colonial one, noting only the "just and legitimate aspirations of the Eritrean people for independence." (The OLF does, however, see the Tigray and Oromo struggles similarly, as the result of the historically necessary struggle of oppressed nations within the Ethiopian empire-state.)

One TPLF publication put the TPLF viewpoint in historical perspective:

> Through deception, intrigue, and outright annexation of the feudal class, the present Ethiopian multination state was born at the latter half of the nineteenth century. And since then the aspirations of the oppressed nations and nationalities, and the Amhara ruling class's need to subjugate them, have vigorously clashed, resulting in numerous political and armed confrontations. The national subjugation has engendered a deep-rooted national contradiction which has manifested [itself] in mutual hostility and mistrust. It is this condition which led to the emergence of independent national organizations representing their respective nations and waging a fierce struggle for self-determination. This being the case, the EPRP's attitude toward these national liberation fronts demonstrated *implicitly* that of liquidationism.[18]

Nonetheless, the TPLF and its supporting organizations have stated that the EPRP has made a contribution to the development of political consciousness and regarded it as a democratic force. Accordingly, the TPLF was ready from the outset to embrace the idea of a united front. The EPRP, which had grouped units of its army in a mountainous area of Tigray called Asimba, had no such sentiments of solidarity, however, and waged a continuous propaganda campaign against the TPLF—calling it "narrowly nationalist," "secessionist," "petty bourgeois," and "fascist"— in order to isolate the TPLF at the national and international levels, and ultimately to eliminate it.

Eventually the TPLF/EPRP dispute erupted into open warfare, despite attempts by the EPLF to mediate in the spring of 1976. In 1977 the TPLF claimed that some of its urban cadres had been betrayed by the EPRP and caught by the Dergue, and that from its Asimba base the EPRP was conducting a campaign to undermine TPLF.[19] In September 1977, learning that the EPRP was preparing to mount an all-out armed attack, the TPLF made vigorous attempts to open a dialogue between the two organizations. The attempt was not reciprocated; and in February 1978 the EPRP launched its armed attack. Its army was quickly defeated by the TPLF and retreated in disarray to ELF-held areas in southwestern Eritrea.[20]

Viewed in the context of events occurring in the region at the time, the EPRP's ill-conceived assault can be seen as an attempt to gain power quickly not only in Tigray but in Ethiopia as well. The timing is instructive. The Dergue had, since the summer of 1977, suffered a series of defeats in Eritrea and the Ogaden, where its army and militia were pinned down. In central Ethiopia, and especially in Addis Ababa, its terror campaign had led it to the heights of unpopularity. Clearly, the EPRP considered this an opportune moment to launch its attack. The result was hardly what it had hoped. It was defeated, both militarily and in the eyes of its supporters, who realized its opportunism. Coming as it did in the wake of the TPLF victory over the EDU, the TPLF was thenceforward able to organize the Tigrean people, unencumbered by the need to counter the political and ideological confusion engendered by outsiders.

The TPLF's awareness of this advantage and increased sense of purpose are evident in its writings—as well as its bold attacks on the Dergue's armed units, and its opening of a second (southern) front in 1979. It states categorically that its efforts to conciliate the difference between the two organizations, and the defensive nature of its military struggle against the EPRP, mark it as an authentic revolutionary force. It also believes that in exposing the EPRP's false claims and counter-revolutionary designs, it has played an important role in advancing Ethiopia's revolution—and that the EPRP's demise has purged the Ethiopian revolution of a dangerous organization that misled thousands of Ethiopian youth, especially abroad.

These claims are endorsed by the analysis made at a seminar organized at the instigation of forty-one EPRP members who had surrendered to the TPLF in February 1978. The seminar produced a penetrating and sober analysis of the EPRP's strategic errors, which was summarized in *Weyyin*, the TPLF monthly, in Amharic. The EPRP's position on the TPLF and other national liberation fronts was analyzed as follows:

(a) It [EPRP] suffered from an organizational chauvinism; (b) it gave priority to urban struggle, overestimating its strength and presenting itself as capable of taking power alone; (c) it had an incorrect line on the national question, being unwilling to regard national organizations as revolutionary forces; as a result it was not ready to take concrete steps toward the formation of a united front. . . .

Because it was not ready to call upon organizations that believed in armed struggle and to make a principled agreement with them, it fanatically relied on a shortcut to power through a *coup d'état*. While paying lip service to a united front, in actual fact it was engaged in armed struggle against revolutionary forces.[21]

The TPLF's victory over the EPRP has enabled it to turn its attention to the main enemy, the Dergue. In the summer of 1978 it mounted a series of lightning attacks on Dergue outposts, destroyed several units and captured a vast amount of arms, ammunition, and other material.[22] In 1979 it captured some important towns, including Maichew, and established a base in the critical mountain region of Amba Alaghe, giving it control of the road from Addis Ababa north to Tigray and Eritrea.[23]

The TPLF's struggle against the Dergue cannot, however, be limited to military activities. The Dergue's control of the media, particularly the radio, enables it to broadcast vilifications of the TPLF and of other liberation fronts, much as the EPRP has done. The TPLF has answered the challenge in a series of pamphlets and leaflets that expose the political bankruptcy of the Dergue.[24] At the same time, the TPLF began to train cadres from the peasantry and form cells in urban areas. Land reform has been carried out in TPLF-held areas, which has solidified the base among the peasantry, as have newly introduced medical and educational programs. Even during the Dergue's latest counteroffensive, the TPLF was able to depend on the peasantry for material support and intelligence. The land reform has been accompanied and reinforced by administrative changes that have established local peoples' assemblies through which they run their own affairs.

The TPLF held its first congress in the field in the spring of 1979. A similar congress is to convene every three years and to elect a central committee as the highest body between any two congresses. The central committee is in turn to elect a political bureau to manage the day-to-day activities of the front.

The achievements of the TPLF over the last five years are impressive. It has organized and politicized the mass of the peasantry in most parts of Tigray. It has developed an underground cellular organization in the cities, through which it can reach its urban supporters. It provides significant, if limited, educational and health services to the people, and it has distributed land and organized cooperative production in the rural areas. It has mobilized and armed a small militia that has played a critical role in the defense of the liberated areas, and has acted as an auxiliary to the TPLF army. It shares with the EPLF, among other things, a belief in self-reliance as a basic goal and operational guide. Eritreans have provided the TPLF with inspiration, encouragement, and material support, while the Tigreans have in turn supported the Eritrean struggle. The wedge between them has been replaced by a more realistic appraisal of the two nations' interdependence and the need for mutual support in the face of their more powerful armed oppressor. The needs of the Tigrean liberation struggle are nevertheless great, and there are no illusions about the pain and sacrifice that will be necessary before the final victory.

# 5

## Somalia
## and the "Lost Territories"

### The History of the "Lost Territories"

The Republic of Somalia is made up of what was Italian Somaliland, which bordered the Indian Ocean, and the former British Somaliland, which bordered the Gulf of Aden and Djibouti. The two were united in 1960 as the result of popular insistence on union that some members of the newly elected government had tried to thwart. The new republic set itself the task of recovering the "lost territories": the Ogaden (which is also known as Western Somalia), Djibouti, and the Northern Frontier District (NFD). Djibouti was then the French colony of the Overseas Territory of the Afars and Issas, the Ogaden was (as it is still) a part of Ethiopia, and the NFD was (as it too still is) a part of Kenya. To symbolize this historic mission, the Somali flag was emblazoned with five stars, each representing one part of the greater Somali nation.

Underlying the territorial claim, which was based on historical, ethnic, linguistic, and cultural continuities, was the extraordinary phenomenon of Somali nationalism, which encompassed all Somali, both in Somalia and in the "lost territories." Somalia's defiance of the African postcolonial order, which the rest of Africa has accepted as the inevitable result of the colonial past, has been bold and heroic. It is therefore important to understand its roots, and how its has been able to survive both European colonial rule and the Ethiopian imperial experience.

97

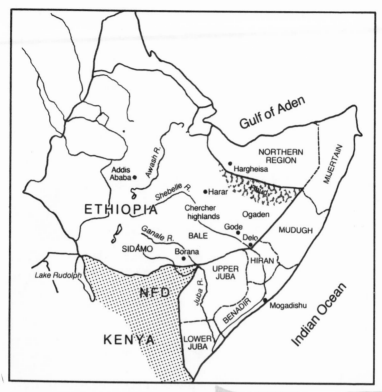

First, and particularly important, Somalia is the only state in
Africa all of whose members share a history, language, and
culture. People known as Somali appear in accounts of the
region going back several centuries, along with related peoples,
including the Afar and the Oromo. Their specific origins are the
subject of speculation, however. The name may be a combination of "so" (go) and "mal" (milk), and would then be based on
its pastoral economy, or it may be the name of an ancient chief or
patriarch,[1] which would be consonant with Somali clan practice
of claiming a common ancestor. Another authority, however,
speculates that:

> One possibility is that they are descendants of Hamitic people
> who arrived in the area after the Oromos. Another theory is that
> the Somalis are actually Semiticized Oromos, the descendants of

the Oromo tribes which inhabited portions of what is now the Northern Region of the Somali Republic and which were subject to influences emanating from Arabia, both through a certain degree of intermarriage and through the adoption of Islam.[2]

The prevailing view, supported by linguistic and other evidence, favors Hamitic origins.

The Somali are subdivided into clans (sometimes also called tribes), each with a specific name and clan (or "tribal") mark, called a *sumad*. Each clan is considered to be the landholding unit of a specific territory, and although each has a chief, his power is restricted to matters concerning the group as a whole.[3] Thus the Ogaden is so-named for the Ogaden clan of the Somali nation whose members inhabited the area. The Somali belief in a common ancestry has been the basis of their national solidarity; Somalis, wherever they have lived, have carried with them an oral tradition in legend and song that celebrates the deeds of folk heroes and records the history of the people. Every colonizer of the Somali has had to contend with the nationalist feeling this process has engendered.

Second, Islam has played an important role in reinforcing Somali national solidarity. For instance, Somali resistance to colonial intrusion was shaped and inspired by the heroic exploits of Mohammed Abdille Hassan, cynically nicknamed the "mad mullah" by the British, who kept the fire of nationalist feeling burning throughout the colonial period, after the British, French, Italians, and Ethiopians had carved up the Somali region. From the early 1900s until his death in 1920, he fought them all— sometimes at the same time—and remained undefeated. His people were able to move about the area, quickly crossing the borders set up by the colonial powers. His deeds are celebrated and he himself was a poet whose imagery had tremendous power: in one poem he likened the colonial powers to "vultures hovering over my head, eager to dip their filthy beaks into my body."

When Menelik began his move to conquer the southern region in the 1890s, he first fought the armies of the Muslim emirate of Harar under Emir Abdullahi, and his defeat of Abdullahi at the battle of Chelenko brought an end to four hundred years of virtually uninterrupted rule. The Harar emirate, northwest of the Ogaden, was a small but separate nation that had used its strategic position astride the trade routes from the interior to the gulf of Aden to build a thriving economy. It was composed of a minority ruling group known as the Adere (or Harari), who had built a network of alliances with other groups, including Somali and Oromo, all of whom paid tribute to the emirate. Islam united these groups and played an important role in cementing opposition to the Christian Menelik. The walled city of Harar was considered a holy city by the Muslims and its capture by Christians thus added religious animosity to anti-Ethiopian sentiment. The French traveler and writer Henri de Monfreid, who worked for Menelik, tells a story that illustrates this: when Menelik received an emissary from Abdullahi on the eve of the battle of Chelenko, the emissary brought a Muslim turban, along with the message that if Menelik wore the turban, the emir's troops would not harm him; if not, then—by Allah!—the emir would tie up him and his men with ropes and dispose of them as he saw fit. Menelik replied that he would wear the turban until the good Lord Medhane Alem (the savior of the world) granted him victory, and he would then stand on the top of the minaret on the central mosque, urinate on it, demolish the mosque, and there build the church of Medhane Alem in its place.[4] Menelik was a man of his word, for the church stands there today.

Although this act was clearly designed to put the finishing touches on the defeat of the Adere, they nevertheless managed to preserve their language and culture by confining themselves to the walled city—a solution that also suited the conqueror's security considerations. And so a small nation, now numbering some 30,000, survived.

After his victory, Menelik placed his cousin Ras Mekonnen (Haile Selassie's father) in charge of consolidating and expanding from the base of Harar. Mekonnen fulfilled his imperial mission by setting up military garrisons throughout the Ogaden, and thus extending the Ethiopian empire to its present border with Somalia. This task was well under way in 1896 when Menelik's forces defeated the Italians at the battle of Adwa.

The three European colonial powers continued jockeying for territory in the Horn. The Italians, who would have liked to extend their Indian Ocean colony of Somalia into the interior and their Eritrean colony southward, had to remain content with what they had—at least until Mussolini's short-lived adventure in the mid-1930s. The precise boundary remains open to question, however, for although it was supposedly demarcated on von Habenicht's 1891 map, and although both sides retained copies, no one seems to know their whereabouts. A convention signed by Italy and Ethiopia in 1908 marked the boundary between Italian Somaliland and the Ogaden and thus covered the northern area, but left a major section of the border unclear.

The British at first claimed only a comparatively small piece of Somali territory, which they used as a supply station for the British garrison at the port of Aden, as well as grazing rights in the fertile area across the border in Ogaden known as the Haud.[5] The British then attempted to make the Haud a protectorate, but were prevented from doing so by Menelik, who, with a garrison entrenched in the Ogaden and the victory at Adwa behind him, was able to negotiate a treaty that confined the British to British Somaliland. The border was thus officially sanctioned in the Anglo-Ethiopian Treaty of 1897, and the British only sought Ethiopian assurance that "Somalis who by boundary arrangement became subjects of Ethiopia shall be well treated and have orderly government."[6]

The French claimed Djibouti as part of their dream of linking French territories in East Africa to French territories on the Atlantic Ocean, but, frustrated by British countermoves, were unable to extend their control inland. They finally agreed to withdraw their frontier to within about one-hundred kilometers of the ocean, thus limiting themselves to the present Djibouti state—even though in 1885 they had signed a treaty with the Issa Somali, who inhabited areas further inland, whereby they agreed to protect them. They then proceeded to develop the port of Djibouti, and signed an agreement with Menelik which provided French financial capital and management for a Djibouti–Addis Ababa railway. The era of Western imperial incursion into Ethiopia thus began.

**The Postwar Territorial Situation**

The story of the post-1941 occupation and liberation of Somali territories forms the immediate background for contemporary Somali nationalism. When Italy was defeated in 1941 and Haile Selassie returned to the throne, the British were divided as to what course to follow. In a statement made before the House of Commons on February 4, 1941, Anthony Eden, then foreign secretary, appeared to favor Ethiopian control over all the territory claimed by Menelik, including the Ogaden:

> His Majesty's government would welcome the appearance of an independent Ethiopian state and recognizes the claim of Emperor Haile Selassie to the throne. The Emperor has intimated to His Majesty's Government that he will need outside guidance. His Majesty's Government agrees with this view and considers that any such assistance and guidance in economic and political matters should be the subject of international agreement at the conclusion of peace. They reaffirm that they have themselves no territorial ambitions in Abyssinia. In the meanwhile the conduct of military operations by Imperial forces in parts of Abyssinia will require temporary measures of military guidance and control. These will be carried out in consultation with the Emperor, and will be brought to an end as soon as the situation permits.[7]

This statement should be read in the light of Britain's regret at its inability to stop the Italian invasion of Ethiopia—a failure that had provoked massive demonstrations in England after Haile Selassie appealed to the League of Nations in Geneva.

Eden's statement was a prelude to an Anglo-Ethiopian agreement signed on January 31, 1942, which recognized Ethiopian sovereignty over the Ogaden, but gave the British administrative control over the strategic city of Jijiga, the agricultural areas around it (the Reserve Areas) and the Haud, and the railway line from Dire Dawa to the border of French Somaliland. The British control of Jijiga and its surrounding areas, as well as the railway, was presumably motivated by the need to prosecute the war still raging in northern Africa and Europe—and also, perhaps, by a colonial rationale, despite Eden's protestations to the contrary. Not surprisingly, Haile Selassie was not pleased with the British presence in the area and continued to maneuver for their complete withdrawal—at this point he was increasingly looking to the United States as the new guardian of his interests. The British responded by gradually reducing their adminstrative presence in the Reserve Areas and allowing the Ethiopian flag to fly beside the Union Jack on government buildings. In 1948 they withdrew almost completely, leaving all of the Ogaden save the Haud in Ethiopian hands; the Haud was relinquished in 1954.

The disposition of the other Somali territories was decided at different times and by different means. With the defeat of Italy, the fate of the ex-Italian Somaliland, Eritrea, and Libya became the subject of international debate. The Allies did not necessarily agree: France, for example, suggested that Italian Somaliland should remain under Italian rule, while the United States proposed direct international administration (which would have meant indirect U.S. control) and the British proposed Somali self-determination in the future—a notable departure from Eden's policies, and attributable to the influence of Ernest Bevin, then foreign secretary of the Labour government. Bevin expressed the British position in a debate in the House of Commons on June 4, 1946:

> In the latter part of the last century the Horn of Africa was divided between Great Britain, France, and Italy. At about the same time we occupied our part, the Ethiopians occupied an inland area which is a grazing ground for six months of the year. Similarly, the nomads of Italian Somaliland must cross the existing frontiers in search of grass. In all innocence, therefore, we proposed that British Somaliland, Italian Somaliland, and the adjacent part of Ethiopia, if Ethiopia agreed, should be lumped together as a trust territory, so that the nomads should have their frugal existence with the least possible hindrance and there might be a real chance of a decent economic life, as understood in that territory.[8]

The Bevin plan of reuniting the Somali territories failed to gain adherents, particularly as British influence in the area, and in international politics, declined and as the United States increasingly backed Ethiopia (it will be remembered that it was in 1952 that the U.S.-backed federation of Eritrea and Ethiopia was finalized). The British withdrawal from the Ogaden was followed by a strengthening of Ethiopian garrisons and the takeover by Ethiopians of provincial administrative offices. Somali nationalism, encouraged by the Bevin plan and given organizational form by the Somali Youth League (SYL), which opened branches throughout all the former colonial territories, was temporarily brought to a halt when the organization was banned.

In 1950 the UN decided to place Italian Somaliland under a ten-year UN trusteeship, with Italy as the administering authority, after which it would become independent. The border dispute, however, had still not been resolved. On December 31, 1958, the UN General Assembly passed a resolution urging the Italian government (as administering authority) and the Ethiopian government to find a solution to the problem. A mediation attempt led by Trygve Lie, former UN secretary-general, failed to produce any positive results, and the disputing parties were unpersuaded by the extensive UN debate that took place in December 1959. The first Somali prime minister, Abdullahi Issa Mohammed, addressed the issue before the Somali legislative assembly on June 26, 1959:

> On the burning question of the border between Somalia and Ethiopia, we have lately actively followed procedures relative to the resolution of the problem. We must admit that despite our most earnest desire, the right steps leading to the solution of this problem have not been taken, and not for lack of good will on our part or on the part of the Italian government. The government of Somalia will do its utmost to resolve this much debated and overdue problem at the earliest time possible, naturally before the end of the [UN] trusteeship, *hoping that account should definitely be taken of an eventual solution based on the aspirations and self-determination of the peoples involved.*[9]

This statement reflects both Somali ambiguity about the extent of its territorial claim and clarity on the question of self-determination. While it does not specify the frontier at which the claims stop, it is unequivocal as to the means by which the Somali peoples in these areas are to express their aspirations. The international community, dominated by the United States, failed to address the issue of self-determination for the Somali in these areas, who were left no alternative but to fight.

Somalia and Ethiopia were soon involved in border conflicts. A major armed clash took place early in 1961, in the wake of the abortive *coup d'état* against Haile Selassie, followed by another in the spring of 1964. On both occasions, an ill-equipped, ill-prepared Somali army was defeated by a larger, better armed, and more experienced Ethiopian force which also had air support. Diplomatically, the 1964 OAU-Cairo resolution put an end to Somali hopes for a settlement based on a UN- (or OAU-) supervised referendum.

### The Resistance Struggle in the Ogaden

The early phase of the Ogaden Somali resistance struggle, dominated by Mohammed Abdille Hassan, has already been described. With his death in 1920, the movement continued, but in a somewhat subdued form, until the departure of the European colonial powers. The second phase began with the Anglo-Ethiopian Treaty of 1948 and ended with the emergence of an independent republic of Somalia in 1960. The roots of the struggle in the Ogaden thus run deeper and go back earlier in time than any national liberation struggle in the Horn, except the Eritrean. The ecology of the region—most of which consists of arid and semi-arid plateau over 2,000 meters above sea level—is suited to pastoralism, and most of the 1 million inhabitants are nomadic herders. What little settled agriculture there is consists of subsistence farming in the fertile plains of the Shebelle river valley and in the edges of the Hararghe highlands. Such a way of life engendered a fierce spirit of autonomy among the Somali, which made them unlikely candidates for Haile Selassie's attempts at "integration." This was further undermined by the emperor's own lack of foresight or planning in instituting his grand designs. When there was an attempt to settle Somali pastoralists at Gode in the Shebelle river valley, beginning in the mid-1960s, a huge church, an equally huge mosque, an elementary school, an expensive provincial administrative complex with fashionable residential villas and an assortment of other buildings were all constructed at enormous public expense, but with little attention being paid to the infrastructure that was necessary for them to function. The minister of public works was put in charge, under the emperor's personal supervision, but without consultation or coordination with the ministries of education, health, or communications. When the buildings were completed there were no roads linking them, no telephone service, no water, and an insufficiently prepared educational and health staff. Above all there was no plan or program aimed at making these new facilities available to the local population. The Somali inhabitants, whose "integration" the project was supposed to bring about, had been forgotten once the bureaucratic process had been set in motion. There were token schools and clinics, with token Somali district administrators, but the military-bureaucratic complex appropriated the lion's share of the budget, with well-intentioned agricultural experts left to do what they could—which was never enough.[10]

Part of Haile Selassie's "integration" program was aimed at social integration through intermarriage. He often ranted and raved at his governors and generals for not taking the initiative in this, refusing to acknowledge the social and cultural gap dividing the Somali from the Amhara—not least among such gaps being religion. His repeatedly paraphrased dictum was that the best way to a man's heart is through his stomach: "Tell your idle wives to teach Somali young women how to cook Ethiopian food and make *tella* [beer], and religion will not be an obstacle." The chauvinism implicit in this imperial command was two-edged: not only were Somali women presumed not to know how to cook, but only Amhara men (mostly soldiers) were to marry Somali women. Such chauvinism only fueled Somali resistance.

The present phase of the struggle began with the establishment of the Somali republic, and the creation of the WSLF immediately thereafter. With headquarters in Mogadishu, early WSLF efforts concentrated on the recruitment of Somali youth living in the Ogaden and elsewhere for military training.[11] It immediately engaged in skirmishes with the Ethiopian army, scoring victories in the Bale area, which is inhabited by both Somali and Oromo, many of whom speak Somali. The Islam religion was a further strong tie, buttressing the common hatred of the forces of occupation. Then, in 1963, Somali in the south-western corner of Bale revolted, followed by Oromo in other areas of Bale, and, in April 1964, by Oromo in the Wabi district. Successful raids against Ethiopian army garrisons and police outposts spread to the district of Delo. By the end of 1965 virtually the whole of the central area of Bale province, except for the towns of Ginir and Garoe, was controlled by "rebel" forces.[12]

Most of the leaders of the Bale revolt were minor officials or local *balabats,* such as the influential Hajji Yisihag of Rayitu, a *balabat* of Wabi who had spent some time in Somalia. In Delo and Ganale the leaders were Wako Gutu, Wako Lugo, and Ahije Chivi, all men of great influence in their areas who maintained close contact with each other. Wako Gutu eventually emerged as the overall leader, responsible for much of the planning and execution of the guerrilla attacks, for coordinating the spread of the revolt across Bale and into the Borana region in southern Ethiopia, and for holding the Oromo and Somali together, but the others retained a considerable degree of autonomy. Despite these auspicious beginnings, and despite spectacular victories over a much better armed and larger imperial army, in the end the Bale revolt collapsed. Wako Gutu surrendered to the imperial government in 1970, under amnesty terms mediated by General Jagama Kello, a Christianized Oromo from Shoa province who had been appointed military governor of Bale toward the end of the revolt. Wako Lugo had surrendered a month earlier, and as the leadership gave up, large numbers of the rank and file melted away to their villages.

The experience of the earlier activities of the WSLF, between 1963 and 1969, and the surrender of Wako Lugo and Wako Gutu raise two questions that remain of current significance. The first concerns the relationship between the WSLF and the Somali government, and the second concerns the relationship between the Oromo liberation movement and both the WSLF and the Somali government. It is not clear, for instance, why Wako Gutu in particular surrendered. One reason may have had to do with supply problems, but probably more important was the lack of a clear strategy, either nationalist or revolutionary, as well as a resulting uncertainty about the compatibility of Oromo and Somali aims.

In the absence of direct and clear evidence, it is possible that the Somali government of the time may have demanded that the revolt be subordinated to Somali objectives, which Wako Gutu was unwilling or unable to accept. He realized, however, the practical necessity of gaining Somali assistance, and his seal carried the legend "General of Western Somalia," lending credence to the hypothesis, while the movement was called the Western Somalia Liberation Front (WSLF). Further, WSLF guerrilla forces were involved alongside Oromo forces at battles in Dolo in February 1967, and the order and discipline with which they withdrew was evidence of a well-trained army that was able to regroup quickly and then carry on harassment tactics from its base area in the deeply forested mountains of Delo. The WSLF maintained a base there, in Ganale, and in parts of Chercher highlands in Hararghe and Arusi, and carried out sporadic guerrilla activities until 1972. Thus at least until that time, the WSLF contained within its ranks Oromo and Somali, united by their common oppression and not acutely divided along national lines.

Nevertheless, the Bale revolt has not been regarded as part of the Ogaden Somali's national liberation struggle, but as part of the Oromo struggle. The problem arises from the fact that early WSLF documents claimed that Western Somalia embraces Bale, Sidamo, Arusi, and Hararghe provinces, not all of which are inhabited only by Somalis. The documents avoid the problem by referring to "the majority of inhabitants [belonging] to nationalities almost analogous with the Somali territory and linked by the religious bond."

After a military coup in Somalia in October 1969, the new government, led by Siad Barre, was at first unable or unwilling to support the WSLF. Supplies of arms and ammunition began to drop off, and several WSLF leaders were detained. Then a new front, calling itself the Ethiopian National Liberation Front, appeared, all of its members united in their opposition to the Somali claim to the areas listed above. This group did not succeed in creating a solid base for itself, but only appeared briefly in the Chercher highlands before it disappeared. A rump leadership maintained an office in Aden until late in 1976, before the emergence of the alliance between Aden and Addis Ababa. Those who remained in Chercher joined forces with the OLF, after the latter had opened its base for armed struggle in the area.

## The New WSLF and Somali Aims

It was not until the WSLF congress at Fik, outside Harar, in January 1976, that an attempt was made to resolve the Oromo-Somali contradictions. According to WSLF sources, it divided into two wings: the "Wariya" wing, which was to represent the Somali inhabitants of the Ogaden, and the "Abbo" wing, which was to represent those living in Bale, Arusi, and Sidamo. Implicit in this arrangement was the claim that the majority of the inhabitants of these later provinces are Somali, and that of those remaining who were classified as Oromo, most were in fact members of a Somali linguistic group that used the word *abbo* rather than *wariya* for "you."[13] This assertion vastly increased the WSLF's territorial demands, and introduced a new dimension into the struggle in the Horn. It also had the ironic effect of unifying Ethiopians behind the beleaguered Dergue.

The leader of the Wariya wing, Abdullahi Hassan Mahmoud, was born in Jijiga, and his deputy, Sherif Hassen Mohammed, was born in Dagabur near Jijiga. They were both teenagers when the Somali Youth League (SYL) was actively organizing in the Jijiga area, and they thus represent a new generation of Ogaden Somali leadership—those born in the Ogaden but educated or militarily trained in Somalia or elsewhere. Abdullahi, for instance, studied at Cairo University, while Sherif was a teacher in Dagabur until he became a guerrilla leader in 1963.

The leader of the Abbo wing is the former Oromo leader Wako Gutu, who began to use the name Ibrahim Waago Gutu Usu, and apparently became a supporter of the liberation of "western Somalia." It is not clear whether Wako had renounced his Oromo origins or whether—once again—he was following a tactical line, dictated by military and political necessity. It is clear, however, that he does not favor an unconditional union of "western Somalia" with the Republic of Somalia, should the former gain independence. Thus while he has stated that the decision about whether the Abbo wing would favor the eventual unification of Bale, Sidamo, and Arusi with Somalia, or their separate independence, will be decided by the people themselves after their liberation, Wariya leaders claimed that the entire region east of the Awash river should be joined to Somalia. These divergent views reveal other differences underlying the Somali/Oromo contradiction. Wako Gutu's democratic answer—leaving it to the people to make a decision after independence—is not only theoretically more appealing but makes greater practical sense. It does not preclude cooperation with, or assistance from, the Siad regime, and is compatible with the basic demand of the Somali government for self-determination for the people of the Ogaden. On the other hand, no matter what Wako Gutu now calls the inhabitants of the region, the question of solidarity with the Oromo has not as yet been openly confronted and clearly articulated.

The 1973–1974 drought had considerably reduced guerrilla activities in the Ogaden, which opened up opportunities for both the Somali government and the WSLF. The WSLF began to demand massive aid for renewed guerrilla assaults, but the Siad regime was divided in two on the issue of intervention. One faction advocated that it be immediate and massive, while the other, led by Siad himself, counseled caution and patience, arguing that the empire was tottering and would fall of its own weight. Guerrilla activity was nonetheless stepped up, due to a sharpened awareness that the imperial regime should be attacked before it recovered its authority. Then Haile Selassie fell and the Dergue emerged. The Dergue promised local autonomy to the different "nationalities," a promise that, as we have seen, was not fulfilled. The Dergue's army was being defeated in Eritrea and struggles within Ethiopia were also undermining its effectiveness.

It was at this point that the now famous Somali songs began to be heard, taunting and ridiculing the Siad regime. The Somali army, which contains a significant number of Somalis from the

Ogaden, began to put additional pressure on the government. Siad had to choose between endorsing open armed intervention, on the side of the WSLF, or offering only covert military assistance. When, in March 1977, the restructured and reinforced WSLF began to meet with success in its new initiative, Fidel Castro arranged a meeting between Siad and Mengistu in Aden. According to Siad, Mengistu refused to discuss issues, simply restating that there was no territorial problem and therefore nothing to discuss.[14] A Soviet proposal for a federation of Ethiopia, Somalia, and the People's Democratic Republic of Yemen (Aden) was then discussed, but Siad's response was that this should be preceded by referenda in Eritrea and in the Ogaden, and that these two territories, should they choose independence, should then join the federation as equal partners. According to Somali sources, Mengistu rejected this proposal. Nevertheless, Siad is reported to have pledged that his government would not take military action to resolve the dispute in the Ogaden.[15]

## Djibouti

In June 1977, Djibouti achieved independence after 115 years of French rule. The French presence in the area—as other colonial presences—was regarded by the Somali as an obstacle to their cause, and the French departure was therefore of great moment. As James MacManus commented before the event:

> From talks with a number of senior Somali officials in Mogadishu, one gains the strong impression that this small nation of around four million people has sensed the opening of an opportunity to reverse the judgment of history and rapidly regain two of the three "lost territories" which in Somali eyes form an integral part of their country. Although no official will publicly say so, there is a firm belief in Mogadishu that the French withdrawal from the Horn next year will bring Djibouti back into the Somali fold by a political rather than military process within a few years of independence next June. Equally, the Somali government is watching

what it regards as the disintegration of the Ethiopian regime in the fascinated certainty that if Ethiopia falls apart, the claimed area of the Ogaden will quietly fall into Somali lap.[16]

Publicly, however, the Somali government stated that it would recognize Djibouti as a sovereign state, and that the historic claim that Djibouti was a "lost territory" would not prevent this. The logic behind the Somali assertion was that once the Issa Somali formed a majority of the population (the Somali claim they comprise as much as 80 percent of the population in the capital and a slight majority outside), there would be no need for military confrontation: the demographic weapon was sufficient.

The Ethiopian government disputed these figures, but it also consistently opposed Djibouti's demands for independence,[17] as did the French. But by 1976 the French had reached a tacit understanding with the Somali, who agreed to political autonomy with a continued French military presence.

At its independence, all manner of regimes, including those in Saudi Arabia and Egypt, pledged to guarantee Djibouti's neutrality and viability, with the aid of the French military presence. Neutrality to Saudi Arabia, and its Western allies, meant avoiding the Soviet orbit. But to maintain this neutrality, the commitment of the leadership of the newly independent state had to be secured.

In a referendum held on May 8, 1977, supervised by observers from the OAU and the Arab League, 79 percent (81,770) of all eligible voters turned out, and 92 percent supported independence. In simultaneous elections to the chamber of deputies, 33 Issa, 30 Afar, and 2 Arabs were elected. Hussein Gouled Aptidon, an Issa, became the head of the new state. Writing nine months before independence, MacManus commented on the nature of the new leadership as follows:

> It seems probable that Hussein Gouled, a prominent nationalist in the French territory whose political past suggests an attachment to power rather than principle, will lead to a Somali-oriented nationalist government in Djibouti after independence.[18]

This was hardly a "neutral" leader. The Somali calculation of a political solution to Somali nationalist aims seems to have been well-founded. The question was what decisions this government would make about joining Somalia. But Hussein Gouled could not make this decision in isolation, and to maintain himself in power he and his supporters had to maintain neutrality. There are four elements that Gouled has had to deal with. The first is geographical and ecological. Djibouti consists of 23,000 arid sq. km. and has a population of only 220,000. Devoid of agricultural and mineral resources, it is sandwiched between Ethiopia and Somalia, on the Gulf of Aden. The port, the center of economic activity, has a capacity of 2,000 ships a year, most of which bring in goods to be transshipped into Ethiopia.

The second element, logically connected to the first, is that Ethiopia is necessary for Djibouti's existence, while Djibouti provides Ethiopia with the outlet for over 60 percent of its import-export trade. In other words, the two are vitally interdependent.

The third element is demographic and political, and has already been noted. Although the Issa clearly form the majority, the Afar have been favored by the French, who backed Ali Aref Bourhan, an Afar, as president of the territory for fifteen years in return for his open support of a continued French presence. The Ethiopians have also favored the Afar. The Afar nation is estimated to be about 630,000, over 500,000 of whom live in Wallo, Tigray, and Hararghe provinces, and in Eritrea. These areas, along with Djibouti, have been referred to as the Afar triangle, and Ethiopia has favored their unification as a response to Somali nationalism. The Afar connection with Ethiopia was further cemented by the fact that Ali Aref was a brother-in-law of Sultan Ali Mirah, the ruler of the Afar of Ethiopia—while the ruler of Issa in Ethiopia was Ugaz Hassan Hirsi, who was in the Ethiopian's pay and a protegé of the imperial government.

The fourth element in the Djibouti equation is external interest, including that of the French. Djibouti is strategically important because of its proximity to the Bab el Mandeb, the gateway to the Red Sea. It is the only point between the Mediterranean Sea and the Indian Ocean where there is a Western military presence.

In 1975, the alliance between Ethiopia (now under the Dergue) and the Afar ended when the Afar revolted in protest against Ethiopian control of their land and the continued French presence in the area. France, Ethiopia, and Somalia began to re-appraise their policies, and each realized that their short-term interests would be best served if Djibouti were allowed to achieve independence, rather than be absorbed into either Ethiopia or Somalia.

The French government insisted that its forces would come to the aid of Djibouti if there were aggression by a foreign army, but that they would not take part in maintaining or restoring order; they pledged continued economic assistance at the pre-independence level (over \$142 million a year), as well as technical assistance. French technicians still run the technical services of Djibouti.[19]

The new government of Hussein Gouled then set about safeguarding its only economic resource other than the port—the 770-km. railway to Addis Ababa. It negotiated for the French share in the railway and a revocation of the agreement granting Ethiopia sovereignty over that part of the port of Djibouti at the railway terminus. The new government was able to take such an initiative in part because of alternate aid offered by Arab governments.

It should be clear from this that the leaders of the new Djibouti nation are caught in a tangle of international rivalries and that to maintain their power they must maintain Djibouti's neutrality. Both the Afar and the Issa are divided, those with established interests in Djibouti feeling loyalty to the new state, with others feeling greater loyalty to their nationals across the border. Any union with either Somalia or Ethiopia is not likely to come from the members of the new government or their supporters in the chamber of deputies. If it comes at all, it will come from outside the government, upsetting the carefully constructed balance of interests and turning Djibouti into a hotbed of confrontation; in that event, Ethiopia and Somalia would not be the only protagonists. On the other hand, Somali military successes, particularly in the Ogaden, will undoubtedly have political repercussions in Djibouti. As already noted, the discussion of the Ogaden war, which is taken up in the next chapter, is therefore of relevance to the question of the future of Djibouti.

Cuban troops remain bogged down in the Ogaden, and one wonders how long they will remain as regional gendarmes.

There are questions as to the as yet unresolved policy of the Somali government toward the Ogaden territory, and its attitude toward the WSLF and the OLF. This is related to the Cuban presence because, as noted earlier, Mengistu called upon the Cubans and Russians when faced with Somali armed intervention in pursuit of territorial claims. If Somalia were now to abandon such claims, but without abandoning its right to assist the WSLF's fight for self-determination, there would no longer be any arguable basis for the continued Cuban presence.

The Somali government, with the hindsight of recent history and realizing that its territorial claims have created more enemies than friends, seems to be developing a more subtle strategy. Territorial claims as such have disappeared from official pronouncements—one no longer hears the old slogan of "From Ferfer to Awash"—and the government seems to be limiting its activities to assisting the WSLF in their fight. The Ogaden defeat seems to have persuaded Siad that there is no alternative to a long-drawn-out guerrilla war in the Ogaden, and that the WSLF must be left to wage it on its own, suitably assisted by the Somali government. The WSLF, for its part, seems to have resolved the contradictions inherent in the division of its forces into two wings, and the faction that insisted on integrating WSLF policy with that of the Somali government has lost out to a more independent policy. This does not mean that the WSLF can afford to break with Somalia—this would be neither desirable nor practicable. It does mean, however, that the WSLF has more room to evolve an independent political line based on a protracted people's war.

These developments, along with the growth of the OLF, have also led the Somali to reappraise the Oromo struggle in the areas adjoining the Ogaden. Interviews reveal a greater readiness on the part of the Somali government and the WSLF to recognize the fact of the OLF presence and to readjust past rhetoric on the Oromo question. Of particular importance was the abandonment of the term "Somali/Abbo," referring to the people living in the area adjoining the Ogaden who are predominantly Oromo; they are now referred to simply as the "Abbo people." This was a major step because it implicitly denoted a revision of the idea that the Abbo (i.e., the Oromo) form a part of the Somali nation.

This was followed by the opening of an OLF office in Mogadishu, a step that goes a long way toward resolving the Somali-Oromo contradiction. In interviews, WSLF leaders made it clear that the organization is ready to cooperate with the Oromo struggle. When pressed on the territorial claims and the boundaries of the Ogaden, one WSLF leader said: "I can solemnly assure you that we will not demand an inch of land that is not ours. We are not expansionists. On the other hand, I don't believe that our Oromo brothers would claim land that is not theirs or deny Somalis land which is Somali property." Beyond this, he said, it is unrealistic to chart contesting claims on a map, for the important thing is for the Somali and Oromo to convince each other of their mutual solidarity with deeds. The territorial question will then disappear as a problem. He added that if the Somali government were to help the WSLF on any grounds other than their right to self-determination, it would be interpreted as an expansionist design. On the other hand, if Somalia's support of the WSLF is based on the recognition of their right to self-determination—and not simply on the border dispute—this will be reflected in its actions in relation to the WSLF. He would not elaborate, beyond repeating that only the future will show what happens.[32]

Meanwhile, the Somali revolution entered a new phase with the election of a national parliament in January 1980, the first since the coup of October 1969. There is still only one party, the Somali Revolutionary Socialist Party (SRSP), led by Siad, which screened the candidates; the party itself replaced the all-military Supreme Revolutionary Council in July 1976, as part of the on-going process of demilitarizing the government. At its first congress, a central committee and a party control committee were formed and a party program proclaimed (the Third Charter of 1976, noted earlier).

The achievements of the party and the government are a matter of record. One of the most important has been the writing of the Somali language and the high rate of literacy that this has made possible (over 47 percent, according to some officials). In January 1975, a new family law gave women legal equality with men, and traditional Islamic leaders who tried to obstruct its implementation were tried and executed, to the delight of Somali womanhood and the dismay of conservative Arab governments (notably Saudi Arabia). The SRSP now boasts that 62 percent of its members are women, whose separate organizations, together with those of trade unionists and youth, are the backbone of the regime. These mass organizations are represented on the central committee, on economic and social commissions, and on committees at all levels where their interests are affected.

Despite the regime's achievements, there is still the problem of continuing the gradual demilitarization of the regime, and charges of clan rule and favoritism must be dealt with. The regime seems to be aware of these, however, and of the potential disaffection of the cadre if they are unresolved. The ability of the regime to survive the defeat in the Ogaden, and to absorb the over 1 million refugees who fled to Somalia in the wake of the war, is testimony to its popularity. The Somali nation is still united, and remains solidly behind the right of the Ogaden Somali to self-determination; it seems equally clear that a reversal of the social revolution of the last ten years will not be tolerated.

# Part 2

## The Politics of Intervention

# 6

## The Big Powers and Their Intermediaries

### The Power Game

The conflict in the Horn has involved a rapidly changing series of cross-cutting alliances which has made the outcome uncertain. For example, at one time both the Soviet Union and Israel were on the Ethiopian side, giving considerable military aid, while the Soviet Union also maintained a military presence in Somalia during the earlier part of the Ogaden war, and the Saudis promised unlimited petro-dollar help if the Somali government would give up its socialist policies in favor of Islamic ones. In Eritrea, Soviet-armed Ethiopian troops fought under cover of F-5, MIG-21, and MIG-23 planes, which dropped cluster bombs supplied by Israel. The Cubans, on the other hand, who at one time supported the Eritrean cause, refused to be involved in front-line combat; instead they provided training and logistical support to Ethiopian troops in the earlier phases of the counter-offensive in Eritrea in 1978, and seem to prefer that the Eritrean struggle be resolved through peaceful negotiations.

When the Soviet Union and the Cubans intervened decisively on Ethiopia's side against Somalia in the Ogaden, U.S. hesitation to help Somalia must be understood in terms of the cross-cutting interests: its lack of response must be seen in the light of the situation in the Middle East and in sub-Saharan Africa and the fact that the United States still regards Ethiopia as the prize in the struggle.

Western reactions to the events in the Horn have varied from demands that the West must "stand up" to the Russians, to comments about the "myth" of the superpowers.[1] Russian and Cuban military intervention after 1977 triggered more extreme reactions, because of the threat this posed to Western military and economic interests in the region. Throughout, very little attention has been paid to the welfare of the African people involved in the struggle, to the sources and tragic consequences of the conflict, or to deciding what can be done to alleviate the suffering and provide a framework for a just resolution.

A typical example of this power-game approach is an editorial in the London *Times*, written during the height of the Ogaden war:

> The war between Ethiopia and Somalia faces Western governments with an acute difficulty. . . . Obviously both Western and African interests demand that Ethiopia should not become a Soviet satellite. It is far from certain that this will be the outcome of the present increasingly sanguinary struggle. Circumstances have, however, given the Soviet Union an exceptionally favorable opportunity to play the Angolan game again. The usual calls for mediation and peaceful agreements have been made, and the Security Council may yet be invoked, along with the Organization of African Unity, but the build-up of arms and the vital interests of both sides are now too involved to leave much hope for an early ceasefire or a political solution.[2]

Yet the "calls for mediation" were not made with a sense of immediacy or a concern that the magnitude of the armed conflict warranted. The *Times* editorial reflects the spirit of the time: a cynical resignation to the imperatives of the power game. The other side of this coin has been the failure of international moral and legal principles to mediate between conflicting parties or nations.

The Soviet Union's decision to switch and side with Ethiopia against Somalia caught its rivals by surprise. The decisiveness, speed, and scale of the intervention turned what had been considered a huge gamble into an event with historic consequences.[3] Those who did not see the Russian switch as utterly cynical speculated that, as the London *Times* put it, "The political chaos in Ethiopia might have a revolutionary authenticity suggested by parallels with Russian history."[4] Castro lent credence to such speculations by embracing Mengistu as a true revolutionary,[5] implying that the Ethiopian revolution was more "authentic" than the Somali one, and that Mengistu had better credentials than Siad Barre—a characterization that does not make sense if both revolutions are analyzed in terms of the local circumstances that produced them.

Whatever the motives, it is now clear that the outcome of the struggle in the Horn, at least for the immediate future, will be determined by this foreign intervention. The internationalization of the struggle has altered the pattern of development of the internal struggles by strengthening the hand of the Dergue, which could not have withstood the EPLF assault without United States and Israeli help (until withdrawn in 1976), or have survived the Somali onslaught in 1977 without Soviet and Cuban help.

It now appears that Ethiopia—the big prize in the Horn—has been secured and the empire preserved, but that the Dergue has deepened its dependence on foreign support and has thus put its future up for ransom. At the same time, however, Ethiopia would not be a valuable prize without a coastal region, which helps explain the Soviet reversal of its previous support for the Eritrean cause.[6] Thus when Soviet strategists were preparing the many-phased counteroffensive in Eritrea early in 1978, Pravda announced that the Eritrean struggle was a tool of Western imperialism aimed at weakening Ethiopia and depriving it of outlets to the Red Sea. "In these conditions," Pravda proclaimed, "the Eritrean separatists are involved in a game played by others [and are] objectively helping the realization of imperialist designs."[7]

Obviously, the Eritrean struggle, which Moscow suddenly decided was pro-imperialist, stood in the way of more "strategic" interests. Since it could not be wished away, or otherwise dealt with to fit the reality of changed power relationships, it had to be targeted as "objectively" helping Western imperialist designs. Pravda also sought to invoke the issue of class struggle:

The genuine interests of the population of the province [Eritrea] coincide with the interests of the entire Ethiopian people, which is trying to build life on new principles. . . . The revolutionary forces supported national unity and saw the whole national question in the context of class struggle within the country and the international sphere.[8]

A further insight into Soviet motives can be found in unofficial remarks made by its diplomats in private meetings and at parties. One such diplomat compared international involvement in the Horn to the caucus race in *Alice in Wonderland,* in which there are no explicit rules and anyone may choose to play or not to play.[9] Unlike the caucus race, however, where everyone is a winner, there is no guarantee that anyone will emerge as a winner in the Horn. Another Soviet diplomat, speaking in an Arab capital, said that the "arrogant Eritreans must be slapped left and right" before they will submit.[10]

## Soviet Intervention

We must begin with a brief reference to the Soviet intervention in Angola in 1975, which was both quantitatively and qualitatively different from its involvement in the Horn. In Angola, the MPLA, a long-time ally of the USSR and a beneficiary of Soviet aid in its struggle against Portuguese colonial rule, faced annihilation by South African armed forces which, in alliance with the U.S.-backed UNITA and FNLA, had penetrated deep into Angolan territory. It was these covert CIA activities, now amply documented,[11] along with South African forces bent on destroying the MPLA, that prompted the involvement of Cuban troops, backed by Soviet arms.

The USSR's accurate assessment of the U.S. domestic political scene and the absence of a U.S. counterforce altered the nature of external intervention in Africa and added a new dimension to African politics. The game of superpower "mutual perception"— of guessing what the opponent is likely to do in the face of any given action—has also been affected, and there has begun a period where, according to one lamenting observer, "Owing to the lack of a consensus behind American policy important opportunities were opened to the Soviets, chances on which they probably had not counted so soon."[12]

This made Soviet intervention in the Horn much easier. There have since developed two schools of thought as to how to respond to the "Soviet challenge": one may be called the "Africanist" school, the other the "globalist" school. They are related to the two theories of Soviet strategy in Africa, the "grand design" theory and the "opportunism" theory.[13]

The "grand design" theory holds that recent events in the Horn are a manifestation of the inexorable unfolding of a long-term Soviet strategy that has four major objectives: (1) To spread the political and economic influence of the Soviet Union in a manner consonant with its role as a world power; (2) as a consequence, to diminish or eliminate Western influence and control; (3) to promote Soviet political and strategic interests, especially by developing a worldwide system of naval and air facilities, in order to offset Western nuclear delivery systems (particularly nuclear-powered missile submarines) and to protect Soviet political power; and (4) to counter the ideological and political challenge of the People's Republic of China.[14]

The USSR is believed to be pursuing these strategic goals in Africa through a series of tactical moves which, although they may appear incoherent and contradictory, represent pragmatic ad hoc responses to developments on the African continent. Therefore, how African leaders and governments see and respond to Soviet policies is an important, perhaps crucial, determinant of Moscow's course on the continent.[15]

Turning to the Horn of Africa, the grand design theorists believe that Soviet involvement has altered the "balance of power" decisively in its favor in an area that is the jugular vein of Western economic interests—the Persian Gulf and Arabian peninsula, with its oil wealth, and the Red Sea, with its crucial sea lanes. If the gamble pays off and Somalia is secured again, Soviet strategic naval objectives would be fulfilled.

The second, "opportunism," theory simply asserts that the record of Soviet activities in Africa, particularly in the Horn, does not indicate the existence of a grand design, but is "reactive and opportunistic."[16] As one close observer put it: "The sloppiness and inconsistency accompanying the Soviet leadership's attempts to avoid a split with Mogadishu reflects a lack of planning and vision."[17]

Some proponents of the "opportunism" theory speak of a Soviet strategy of "counter-imperialism," which brings it closer to the grand design theory.[18] On the political plane, this entails emphasis on states and political groups of some inherent geopolitical importance rather than on those which are progressive per se, and the emphasis is on those countries lying in a broad arc to the south of the Soviet border, from North Africa through the Mediterranean and around to South Asia. The "counter-imperialism" doctrine further holds that instead of trying to use economic aid to win political influence, Moscow is increasingly using its own economic strength (plus its political clout) to gain privileged economic positions for itself. Here, too, we see a meeting ground between the two theories. The observer cited earlier thus notes that although the USSR was reacting to developments in the Horn rather than following a carefully drafted plan, the magnitude of the involvement indicated the emergence of a new pattern of Soviet "imperial behavior," involving the use of decisive and brutal power, and having the ability and the will to use it far beyond its traditional sphere of influence. Moreover, according to this analysis the extent of Soviet military involvement represents a break with a traditionally conservative use of military power, in circumstances where neither vital Soviet interests nor prestige are at stake.[19]

## U.S. Involvement

What has U.S. policy toward the conflict of the Horn been? The Carter administration claims that it has avoided direct involvement. If so, is this a new policy of disengagement in an area traditionally the sphere of influence of the United States and its allies? If not, is there a hidden agenda behind this avoidance of direct involvement—a secret Soviet-U.S. entente? Or, as one commentator has put it, is U.S. policy in the Horn "*aboulia* or proxy intervention?"[20]

The reference to *aboulia*—lack of will—is to a charge by Senator Henry Jackson that Carter has lacked the will to play a more active role in Africa. More to the point, however, is the United States' need to keep its options open under the pressure of conflicting priorities in the post-Vietnam era. In this situation, there are two schools of thought as to the U.S. role. The first focuses on African "intractability"—that African nationalism defines African behavior—and predicts that because of this the USSR will fail to establish a lasting zone of influence. At the same time, Soviet-Cuban intervention on the Ethiopian side in order to maintain OAU-sanctioned colonial boundaries will in fact only serve to buttress the neo-colonial legal order, and Soviet-Cuban military support for Ethiopia can be seen as a "stabilizing" influence in the area. The logical conclusion is that since the United States has no alternative to the African political order, it should welcome the role played by Moscow and Havana.[21]

This "Africanist" school, presumably including among its adherents Cyrus Vance and Andrew Young, is pitted against the globalist school under Zbigniew Brzezinski's patronage. This school analyzes the struggle in the Horn from the point of view of overall U.S.-Soviet competitive relations. Soviet involvement in Africa is thus seen as the result of a policy designed to undermine Western (and Chinese) influence, and Africa and the Horn are the board on which the game is played because they offer the ripest opportunities, as well as because of Africa's increasing intrinsic importance. Moscow's search for influence in Africa must be seen in the light of such interests as its access to bases, its proximity to Western shipping lanes, the desire to exploit the racial conflict in Southern Africa at the expense of the West, to deny mineral resources to the West by encouraging Marxist and radical regimes, and to develop a reputation as the only reliable and credible champion of the African causes.[22]

Clearly, the differences are not over fundamental strategic questions, but over tactical responses to the emerging Soviet role in Africa and in the Horn in particular. There is no open clash between the two views; nor has the conflict been resolved with the emergence of a dominant policy line: "Like ships passing in the night, the two sets of assumptions and concerns are seldom obliged to confront each other directly."[23] They reflect a leadership crisis in the Carter administration as much as they do the crisis of U.S. imperialism in the face of a new and powerful challenger to its dominion.

The strategic content of U.S. policy in the Horn must be seen in terms of the Middle East and sub-Saharan Africa, particularly Southern Africa, for two reasons. The first has to do with the position toward the struggle in the Horn adopted by the dominant Arab states, in particular Saudi Arabia and Egypt, and the second with the position expressed in the OAU by the governments of black Africa. U.S.-Arab cooperation in the Horn is determined by a mutual interest in the Arab-Israeli conflict and in the Arabs' long-term policy on oil. As for the African consideration, the African governments' interest in preserving the postcolonial status quo puts them on the side of Ethiopia in the Ogaden conflict, with Somalia viewed as an aggressor bent on upsetting the apple cart. In this respect, the Soviet switch to Ethiopia's side over the Ogaden war stole the tactical political thunder from the United States, and is probably one reason why the United States welshed on its alleged promise to help Siad Barre. The Soviet Union was, after all, implementing a policy of postcolonial "stability" that the U.S. supported. In addition, Soviet support of the liberation forces in Southern Africa lends an air of legitimacy to its intervention in the Horn, while its support of the Palestinian cause adds another.

Andrew Young played a crucial role in the United States' search for an appropriate response to the Soviet Union's challenge. Rejecting Brzezinski's advocacy of a more aggressive attitude, Young (supported by Vance) argued that the Soviet presence in Ethiopia is temporary, and that it is in certain respects beneficial: the Soviet Union has been paying a heavy price in helping to maintian "stability" in Ethiopia and has been taking the blame for its efforts in that respect. In the long run, the USSR will become bogged down in Ethiopia, enmeshed in intractable African national problems, which it does not understand, and will be expelled from there as it was from Egypt, the Sudan, and Somalia. Others in the State Department add hopefully that Ethiopia will become the Russian Vietnam. Thus Brzezinski's belligerent approach, advocating a "linkage" between Soviet policy on Africa and SALT II, for instance, lost out to the "Africanists."

## The Interplay of Interests

After a quarter century of U.S. domination, Ethiopia's neo-colonial bonds seemed to have loosened and revolutionary forces were released in 1974. But the bonds were not completely severed, and Ethiopia continued to receive arms from the United States for its "defense requirements" up until February 1977. Further, there remain economic links with the United States and Europe that must be understood in terms of the strategic interests discussed above: for instance, if the United States cut off aid to Ethiopia, Eritrea might become independent and align with the Arab states, thus posing a threat to Israel, especially to the oil tankers and other ships that pass through the Bab el Mandeb. As long as Somalia was backed by the USSR, arming and economically assisting Ethiopia was a logical countermove and a guarantee of U.S. credibility in the world as a whole and in Africa in particular. After the Soviet switch and the Dergue's expulsion of U.S. military advisory units in 1977, the United States was faced with a crisis. It was at this point that the Young-Vance approach—stay calm, back Ethiopia, and time and Africa will take care of the Soviet Union—seems to have won out, leaving the Somalis out in the cold.

As the table shows, U.S. military aid to the Dergue continued in 1977. In fiscal year 1974 alone, the Dergue received $11 million in U.S. military assistance—half of this type of aid for all Africa—and a further $11 million in military purchase credits.[24] The equivalent figures for 1975 were $11.5 million and $25 million respectively, and in 1976 more aid was given to purchase eight F-5A fighter bombers. As late as the summer of 1976, the

U.S. Military Assistance to Ethiopia

| | Grants (in thousand U.S.$) | Sales (in thousand U.S.$) | Personnel trained in the United States |
|---|---|---|---|
| 1970 | 10,494 | 6 | — |
| 1971 | 11,763 | — | 140 |
| 1972 | 10,645 | 10 | 159 |
| 1973 | 9,439 | — | 156 |
| 1974 | 11,719 | 7,440 | 147 |
| 1975 | 12,999 | 22,127 | 130 |
| 1976 | 7,277 | 135,339 | 192 |

Source: "United States Arms Policies in the Persian Gulf and Red Sea Area," cited in Fred Halliday, "U.S. Policy in the Horn of Africa: *Aboulia* or Proxy Intervention?" *Review of African Political Economy*, no. 10 (September–December 1978), p. 16.

United States had authorized the sale of $6-million worth of military equipment for 1977. Training also continued: in 1976–1977, 190 Ethiopians were trained in the United States. The Dergue also turned to other sources for military supplies, including Iran for F-5A bombers, Israel for cluster bombs and other weapons, and European arms dealers for other materials.

The table reveals two basic facts: First, the United States shifted from grants to substantial sales. Second, the U.S.-Dergue relation increased dramatically—with the total of aid and sales for the two years 1975 and 1976 being almost three times the total for the five years between 1970 and 1974—at the same time that the Dergue was throwing up a smokescreen of anti-imperialist slogans.

With the advent of the massive Soviet arms infusion into Ethiopia beginning in 1977, U.S. aid—through AID and the World Bank—shifted to the economic field. Such support of the Dergue, which enabled it to survive and continue the wars in Eritrea and the Ogaden, was a continuation of Kissinger's concept of measured support in order to forestall Soviet gain. For instance, testifying before the Senate subcommittee on African affairs in August 1976, William Schaufele, assistant secretary of state for African affairs, stated:

We believe we would incur much criticism from our friends in Africa and elsewhere were we to withdraw support for the Ethiopian government during this time of difficulty—such a move would also be attributed to distaste for Ethiopia's brand of socialism.

He added that the Dergue's policies did not lead to systematic opposition to the United States. When asked if he would call the Dergue anti-American, he replied:

No sir, I would not. Certainly in the press there are attacks on the United States but by and large the government, although it is attempting to set up some kind of a leftist or socialist system in Ethiopia, however unfocused and disorganized it may be, is not systematically or instinctively anti-United States. . . . I don't find that the government, despite its sometimes inconsistent attitudes, is basically anti-United States.[25]

There was some dissent, of course, but Halliday points out the paradoxical source of this:

It was the rightist elements inside the U.S. who favored continued support for the Dergue, for the anti-Russian strategic reasons given above, whilst it was the liberals who tended to oppose aid to the Dergue, either on the grounds that the Soviet threat was exaggerated, or could not be countered in this way, or on the grounds that the Dergue, by suppressing the Eritreans and by its summary execution of opponents, was not to be supported on human rights grounds.[26]

Halliday cites Tom Farer as an example of the liberal critics. Farer countered the arguments of the State Department on the grounds that: (1) Neither Eritrea nor the Bab el Mandeb were of particular strategic interest to the United States or Israel; (2) the idea that a U.S. shift would lead to secessions in Africa was untenable; and (3) the political character of the Dergue was alien to the United States, and it was not legitimate to support the Dergue simply because the USSR was backing Somalia.

The Carter administration announced in early 1977 that it would cut military aid (but not sales) to Ethiopia on human rights grounds. This provided an excuse for the pro-Moscow faction within the Dergue, and its allies, to call for a break with the United States. The United States adopted a cautious wait-and-see policy, maintaining relations with the Dergue and not cutting economic aid, but keeping a low profile. Nor was this policy limited to the executive branch of the government. For instance, two congressmen, Don Bonker and Paul Tsongas (a former Peace Corps volunteer in Ethiopia, and now a U.S. senator), visited Ethiopia on a goodwill mission and met Mengistu in November 1977. In late February 1978, the United States announced it was supplying some jeeps and spare parts as part of a $40 million military purchase ordered in May 1977. The United States continued, however, to denounce the Soviet and Cuban role in the Horn.

At the same time, and as if to meet Brzezinski's aggressive line half way, Carter sounded the "globalist" alarm. In a foreign policy statement issued on June 11, 1977, he said: "My own inclination . . . is to aggressively challenge, in a peaceful way of course, the Soviet Union and others for influence in areas of the world that we feel are crucial to us now or potentially crucial fifteen or twenty years from now." Such countries include Vietnam, Iraq, Somalia, Algeria, China, and Cuba. As Ethiopia increasingly came under Soviet influence, Carter instructed Vice-President Mondale to tell Vance and Brzezinski to move to win Somalia's friendship, and it was decided in July 1977 to arm Somalia. According to Arnaud de Borchgrave, the "Somalis claim that they began their all out invasion of the Ogaden region last July [1977] because of the prospect of U.S. arms aid—and because they had received a secret U.S. message [from the "very top"] which they interpreted as a go-ahead to conquer the area."[27] The United States officially denies that such was intended, which, if de Borchgrave is right, reveals the acute contradiction between two conflicting approaches.

The Somalis, using Soviet arms, proceeded to sweep across the Ogaden, only to find that they had no U.S. support. When the Soviet- and Cuban-backed Ethiopian army defeated the Somali army, U.S. diplomats sanctimoniously noted that Somali "aggression" made U.S. aid impossible.[28]

One of the reasons for this withdrawal of the arms offer was the anger that it provoked in Kenya, which feared Somali designs on the NFD if the Ogaden was won. The interests of Kenya, a model of neo-colonial development, could not be sacrificed by the U.S. and British governments, and the Western response to Kenyan protests was unequivocally on Kenya's side.

## Cuba: An Intermediary Power

The major powers are not the only nations interested in the struggle in the Horn. Local or regional powers are also involved, including the Sudan, lying immediately north and northwest; Egypt, Libya, and Israel further north; Saudi Arabia and the People's Democratic Republic of Yemen across the Red Sea and the Gulf of Aden; and Kenya in the south. The Arab-Israeli conflict has also indirectly involved Syria and Iraq, while Cuba has become involved in its attempt to influence the outcome of local struggles.

The interest of most of the neighboring states is due to their evaluation of the alignment of forces involved, and the long-term implications of the outcome, particularly as they may affect their own national interest. It may also reflect the perceptions of the major powers with which each government is aligned. The Cuban intervention cannot, however, be explained in terms of a need to protect Cuba's national interest, because no such interest is directly threatened. There is no historic or geographic factor linking Cuba to the struggle in the Horn, save its earlier support of the Eritrean struggle through training and other facilities. The term "intermediary" is therefore used to distinguish Cuban involvement and is defined as a type of military involvement whereby the intermediary, whatever its motives, intervenes directly to influence or shape the course of events.

Why have the Cubans intervened in the Horn, on whose behalf or for what purpose? Opinions vary, from the extreme rightists who call the Cubans Russian mercenaries, to leftists, who are divided in their assessment of the subject. The Cubans' own perception of their role may be gleaned from statements made by Cuban leaders, including Fidel Castro.[29] From these, it appears that the Cubans see themselves as an internationalist, revolutionary force, advancing, assisting, or defending revolutionary movements. The clearest example was the intervention in Angola in 1975 to defeat an imperialist plot to destroy the MPLA; the left did not hesitate to commend that role. But in the Horn the issue is not as clear as it was in Angola; nor can all the forces involved in the struggle be neatly divided into pro-imperialist and anti-imperialist camps. The central issue is the Cuban view of the Ethiopian regime, and the Cuban perception of forces within and outside Ethiopia as helping, or harming, that regime.

Cuban involvement in the Horn before 1974 was concentrated in Somalia, where a fairly large Cuban group trained and advised the Somali armed forces in the use and maintenance of Soviet weapons and arms. Cuban intervention in Ethiopia on a large scale followed in the footsteps of the Soviet turnaround after 1977, although small groups of advisers had been there since the 1974 revolution.

The Cubans chose to support Ethiopia, and having made that choice did so decisively, particularly during the war in the Ogaden, when between 15,000 and 18,000 Cubans took part in combat, provided logistical support, maintained artillery and rocketry, drove tanks and armored personnel carriers, and flew as pilots of Russian MIG-21s and MIG-23s. The Cubans argued that the Ethiopian revolution was more "authentic" than the Somali one, and that Somalia's invasion of the Ogaden constituted a threat to the Ethiopian revolution. Cuban help in Eritrea had been limited to some logistical support and a token presence in the capital of Asmara to help maintain "law and order." Reports of Cuban troop involvement in front-line combat have not been made recently, although it is suspected that Cuban pilots may be flying MIGs.

The most enthusiastic, and uncritical, view of the Ethiopian revolution comes from Cuban writer Raul Valdes Vivó, who repeats an analysis of Mengistu that was previously expressed by Castro. In a book on Ethiopia, Vivó asks how a revolution can possibly triumph without a party, or without an organized revolutionary movement, but he avoids answering this critical question by simply stating: "The answer to these questions provides a truly great lesson in dialectics," adding that "apart from the mass spontaneous nature . . . the most surprising thing about the Ethiopian revolution was that the leadership was taken by the armed forces. Such a surprise had a hidden logic: it had to be the army or nobody. If not, Ethiopia would have become a society without any social order at all."[30] At the same time, the Cubans are at pains to distinguish the struggle in Eritrea from that in the Ogaden and other parts of Ethiopia. Carlos Rafael Rodríguez, member of the political bureau of the central committee of the Communist Party, vice-president of the council of state and of the council of ministers, and minister of foreign affairs, has emphatically denied Cuban involvement in any attempt to liquidate the Eritrean struggle, and other Cubans claim to have resisted several attempts to involve them directly in the fighting in Eritrea.[31] Mengistu's visit to Havana in April 1978 was principally designed to persuade the Cubans to change their minds and aid Ethiopia against the Eritreans, as they had against the Somali in the Ogaden. Mengistu even tried to go over the heads of the Cuban leadership and appeal directly to the people at a mass rally. The Cubans insist, however, that the Eritrean question is an internal matter, which the parties involved should settle peacefully among themselves, and in this way distinguish it from the Ogaden, where they responded to the urgent call of a sovereign state to help repel a "foreign invasion." At this point, the Cuban perception of the Ethiopian revolution and of its leadership becomes crucial in determining their intervention on its side. For there was Cuban involvement in Somalia before the Ogaden war: Cuban troops advised and helped train the Somali army in the early 1970s, and continued to do so until November 1977, when Siad Barre broke relations with Havana.

Is this "internationalism" the real or the only reason for the Cuban position? Are there not perhaps some aspects of national interest involved? Is there, for instance, a Soviet-Cuban "joint venture," with the Cubans in fact acting to uphold Soviet geopolitical objectives, in partial payment of the "debt" the Cubans owe for military and economic support over the past twenty years? The preponderance of informed opinion on the Cuban intervention in Angola is that they acted as free agents and on their own initiative. There was consultation with the Russians, of course,[32] and at later phases of the Angolan involvement the consultation may have deepened into a more concerted strategy in defense of the Angolan state—although even here there does not appear to have been complete agreement on all issues. But that common involvement in Angola has no doubt provided the two allies with shared perceptions of, and approaches to, African "problems," so that when one decided to become involved on the Ethiopian side, the other may have agreed to fall in line.

So the argument goes. This was borne out during Castro's attempt to mediate between Ethiopia and Somalia by convening a meeting of Mengistu and Siad Barre in Aden in March 1976, where it was proposed that a federation of Ethiopia, Somalia, and the People's Democratic Republic of Yemen be formed. This attempt to create an anti-imperialist front in the region lacked the proper foundations, however. Siad Barre introduced two conditions: first, that the Eritreans be allowed to join the federation as equal partners; and second, that the people of the Ogaden be given the right of self-determination with an option to join the federation. Mengistu rejected both. The failure of the meeting to consider Siad Barre's conditions, or of the mediators to explore alternatives, and their subsequent alignment with Ethiopia while blaming Somalia for the failure of the proposed federation, certainly shows a predisposition toward the Ethiopian side.

Some observers also believe that personality played a not insignificant role at that crucial moment. Siad Barre's more deliberate and pragmatic approach may have dampened the revolutionary ardor of the Cuban leader, whereas Mengistu's eagerness for recognition, which led him to go to any lengths to please, may have invested his enthusiasm with a revolutionary guise. This may partly explain Castro's oft-quoted commendation of Mengistu as an "authentic revolutionary." From that point on, Mengistu's political biography has been partially rewritten, with Vivó painting a picture of him as the architect and helmsman of the Ethiopian revolution. In Vivó's pen, Mengistu's six-month stay in the United States for an ordinance administration course is transmuted into an epoch-shattering experience that changed the course of his life: "Through his experience in the United States, Mengistu began to get a clear view of the present world with its uncontrollable increase of revolutions, rebellions, and conflicts."[33]

As for Cuban national interest in the region, and in Ethiopia in particular, the facts do not bear out this line of reasoning. Cuba's long-term economic goal is to develop an integrated community of Latin American nations. As Castro stated categorically in 1973: "We are Latin Americans. . . . In the future, we should integrate ourselves with Latin America."[34] This policy rests on a shift from what James Petras has called "revolutionary bi-polar politics" to a "regional bloc strategy of isolating the United States."[35] Nor is the Cuban dependence on either the Soviet Union or its Eastern European economic allies (in COMECON) considered so irreversible that the Cubans blindly do Moscow's bidding. A study of Soviet-Cuban trade relations shows that the Soviet share of Cuban imports and exports had fallen considerably by 1974, and that Cuban trade expanded faster with the non-Soviet bloc countries than it did with the Soviet bloc countries between 1971 and 1974. In these years Cuba's total international trade increased by about 89 percent (from 2,374.1 million to 4,443.1 million pesos), while its trade with COMECON expanded only about 69 percent (from 1,373.1 million to 2,325.9 million pesos).[36]

The acid test of Cuba's claim to a revolutionary internationalist role is Eritrea, but the Cuban role is obscured by two conflicting claims. On the one hand, there were reports of a limited Cuban involvement in training the Ethiopian military and providing logistical support during the counteroffensive in the summer of 1978, which resulted in the recapture of several cities by the Ethiopian army. On the other hand, there appear to be Soviet-Cuban differences on Eritrea, manifested in the lack of Cuban involvement in the October–November 1978 counteroffensive which culminated in the recapture of the EPLF-held city of Keren and which was coordinated by about 2,000 high- and middle-ranking Soviet officers and soldiers.[37] Cuba's decision not to be involved in Eritrea, if true, signals a new stage in the struggle there: it will necessitate greater Ethiopian reliance on Soviet personnel for coordinating a protracted war—and it may indeed mean a Soviet Vietnam.

What about the South Yemeni role? Would they step in to replace the Cubans? South Yemeni soldiers were reportedly involved in the Ogaden war on the Ethiopian side, as well as in battles around Massawa in late 1977. But they have since been withdrawn and have apparently pledged not to side against the Eritreans, whom they have supported since the late 1960s. Both the EPLF and the ELF maintain an office in Aden, and did so even when South Yemeni troops were reportedly engaged in battles around Massawa.

## Saudi Arabia: A Surrogate Power

Saudi Arabia, the linch-pin of U.S. policy in the region, is gravely concerned about the struggle in the Horn. The Saudis see the Soviet presence from an anti-Communist perspective, as the United States did during the Nixon administration and to a considerable extent continues to do today. U.S. thinking is inevitably affected by Saudi perceptions of the "Communist danger," and vice versa. As Halliday has put it: "The U.S.A. and the Arab states both need each other, in diplomatic terms vis-à-vis Israel, and in the long-run disposal of oil revenues which these states are earning."[38]

After the death of King Faisal in 1975, the new Saudi ruling group moved steadily toward a more active role in the region, using oil and the financial power derived from its revenue as a weapon. The "recycling of petro-dollars,"—more simply, exporting cash to the Third World through U.S. multinational banks—has further strengthened the Saudis' bonds with the United States, as well as the Saudi ruling class. Saudi Arabia's foreign policy fits well with the U.S. policy of bolstering governments in Africa and the Middle East that share the U.S.-Saudi goal of limiting Soviet and Communist influence. For example, when the U.S. Congress refused to appropriate $150 million to help Zaire's Mobutu confront Angloa in 1976, the Saudis stepped in to give Mobutu the money. And, in the spring of 1977, Saudifinanced Moroccan troops flew to Zaire to help put down a revolt in Shaba province aimed at toppling Mobutu. In Egypt, Saudi financial support of Sadat's regime has enabled him to survive the crises that his chaotic counterrevolutionary policies created.[39]

The Saudi Arabian role is at its most aggressive in its efforts to curb Soviet influence in the Horn and the surrounding region. The Saudis took the initiative in both formulating a plan and putting up the money to get Somalia to break its military alliance with the Soviet Union, which admirably suited the United States in its desire to avoid direct involvement. The Saudis offered Somalia $300 million on condition that it expel the Russians and return to the Islamic fold. The Saudis also regard the "radical" Arab regimes in Iraq, Syria, and South Yemen as Soviet surrogates, and have repeatedly conspired to overthrow them.

The divergence of views on Israel, and especially after the Camp David meetings, has caught the United States in a dilemma, torn as it is between its dependence on Saudi Arabia as a principal source of energy and its commitment to Israel.

Despite Saudi misgivings regarding U.S. handling of the Arab-Israeli conflict at the Camp David meetings, and despite public statements by members of the Saudi ruling groups regarding the U.S. presence in the region, U.S.-Saudi relations are held in a vital bond, with Saudi Arabia acting as a surrogate for the U.S. in the region, as well as assuring a flow of oil to the West, in return for military and other support. The Saudi rulers are convinced that the prospect of a radical overthrow of their government and a loss of control over the oil line to the U.S. market is unacceptable to Washington. As a U.S. foreign service official put it: "For them [the Saudis] American policy toward Saudi Arabia is defined by what American policy toward the family is. That is the strongest commitment they could want."[40]

Nor is oil the sole factor in this alliance. An estimated $40 billion-worth of oil revenues are held in U.S. banks alone, and another $20 billion elsewhere. Saudi Arabia purchased more U.S. treasury bonds in 1977 than did West Germany, the United States' traditional big buyer. It has been estimated that Saudi Arabia's accumulated foreign holdings will reach $100 billion by 1980. The Saudis are clearly conscious of the power implicit in this fact, and it is expressed in interesting ways. Thus the Saudi foreign minister, Saudi bin Faisal called this the "money weapon," which could be used to exert influence in any direction, including by undermining the economy of the capitalist countries.[41] The presumption of U.S. policymakers is obviously that this will not happen, in part because such a move would damage the developing Saudi economy, and would then be contrary to the Saudi government's own interest.

The fall of the Shah of Iran, however, has created some confusion in U.S.-Saudi relations. A statement issued by Saudi bin Faisal seemed to indicate a policy reappraisal in the wake of the Shah's fall and the United States' inability to stem the revolutionary tide. In an interview published in *Al Hawada* (Beirut) on March 3, 1979, he was quoted as saying that he recognized the Soviet Union's "important role in world politics," and that he did not share the U.S. fear of expanding Soviet influence as a destabilizing force in the region, adding that "what threatens the region and its stability is the danger of Zionism." This was, of course, before the Soviet invasion of Afghanistan.

This view may reflect more of a displeasure over U.S. negotiations with Israel than an overture to the Soviet Union. It could also, however, be a tactical ploy to stave off a radical assault on the regime. This would assume a Saudi anxiety over the United States' inability to confront the Soviet Union or its regional allies in the face of an emerging revolutionary upsurge exemplified by the Iranian situation, which has sharpened the Saudi rulers' sense of insecurity. The Saudi foreign minister's statement lends credence to this analysis: "We wish to emphasize that the absence of diplomatic ties [with the USSR] does not mean we do not recognize the Soviet Union. On the contrary, we have often expressed our gratitude for the positive policy adopted by the Soviet Union towards Arab issues."

It is worth noting, however, that Saudi bin Faisal has consistently pursued a line more independent of U.S. policy than has Fahd. There thus appears to be a factional split in the Saudi ruling group, with Saudi bin Faisal representing a minority "left" (or, more appropriately, neutral) group that has been heartened by recent events. This is borne out in Saudi bin Faisal's comments during U.S. Defense Secretary Harold Brown's visit to the area:

> The Americans felt that the Soviet Union is trying to take advantage of the changing conditions in the region. They believe the Soviets are trying to enhance conflicts and encourage violence. They regard this as dangerous because it tends to disturb the international balance. We explained [to Brown] that we have nothing to do with international strategies. . . . What in fact threatens the region and its stability is the Zionist danger. The way to reestablish calm and stability in the area is by having Israel withdraw from the occupied Arab territories, return Jerusalem and recognize the Palestinian people's right to self-determination.[42]

The United States has attempted to reassure the Saudis. Brown's offer to station a U.S. military force in Saudi Arabia was turned down by the Saudi government, but the United States is still eager to demonstrate the importance it attaches to the "stability" of the Persian Gulf, and is considering expansion of U.S. naval forces in the Indian Ocean, including the dispatch of amphibious landing vessels, temporary visits of war planes to the area, and joint military planning arrangements with local armed forces.[43]

Recent events in the region have thus apparently led to a crisis of confidence, as well as a communications gap, between the two strategic allies. If the United States has learned any lesson from recent events, it is that in dealing with the Saudis it cannot overplay its role of guardianship and present the Saudis with a *fait accompli*, particularly on sensitive issues such as Israel.

Moreover, the situation created by the Iraqi-Syrian reconciliation also affected the Saudis' sense of initiative and independence. U.S. officials believe that the Saudi decision to go along with the majority of Arab states in condemning the Camp David agreements was a temporary aberration and that the Saudis have moved away from this position. But the Saudis have nevertheless been critical of Sadat because they are unwilling to break with the other Arab states over the issue of peace with Israel, unless there is a just resolution to the Palestinian question. What the Saudis want is a U.S. security umbrella, without being too closely identified with the United States. This may lead to an increase of ties with Western Europe, as well as a renewal of diplomatic relations with the Soviet Union. In that event, the aggressive surrogate role the Saudis have played in the struggle in the Horn may change to a more low-key "checkbook diplomacy," involving financial largesse.

# 7

## Neighbors and Meddlers

### Arab Interest in the Region

There are four concerns that determine the policies of the Arab governments in the region. First, there is the fear of revolutionary movements and of Soviet influence on such movements. This has been the dominant preoccupation of Egypt and the Sudan, as well as of Saudi Arabia. It has led to attempts to contain the Ethiopian revolutionary upsurge, to stifle the Somali revolutionary experiment, to gain control over the Eritrean struggle and undercut its revolutionary potential in the region, and to encircle the revolutionary government of South Yemen. The attitude of the various countries to each other and to events in the Horn—and their dramatic reversals of position, particularly with regard to Eritrea—must be understood more in terms of each regime's perceived threat to its own survival than in terms of "national" interest, slogans to the contrary notwithstanding.

Second, there is the interest in the Sudan as the meeting ground of African and Arab interests, for it is through the Sudan that events in the Horn most immediately affect the Arab world. The Sudan is Africa's largest country, with 2.5 million sq. km. and a population of only 15 million. Egypt, which has a population of some 40 million and is 97 percent desert, needs access to Sudanese land for its farmers and to Sudanese food for its urban masses. It also wants a friendly state in control of the Nile headwaters. The challenge to any and every relationship be-

tween Sudan and Egypt has been for the latter to overcome the
historic suspicion that it wants hegemony rather than partner-
ship. A strongly emerging pattern of cooperation—highlighted
by a defense pact and a joint parliamentary session held in
Cairo in 1977—emphasized coordination of national programs
in education, health, labor, and social security insurance.

Egypt's historic interest in the Sudan is matched by that of
Saudi Arabia, both as a U.S. surrogate and as a regional Arab
power. The latter aspect is revealed in the oft-cited Saudi plan to
turn the Sudan into an "Arab breadbasket."[1] An Arab Fund for
Economic Development, headquartered in Khartoum, has been
established with Saudi and Kuwaiti financing, and plans to
invest $2.2 billion in the Sudan over the next ten years.[2] By 1985
the Sudan is expected to provide the Arab world with 40 percent

of its food requirements. But the cultural, structural, and infrastructural constraints are too immense to realize such a dream—at any rate by 1985.

The third concern that determines Arab policy in the Horn involves the intentions of the Israeli state in the region. If they could, the Arab states would deny Israel any influence in the Red Sea area, but they were forced by United States and Iranian pressure to permit Israel to import oil from Iran via the Red Sea. After the 1967 and 1973 wars, Israel was successfully isolated diplomatically and economically by the Arab states, and its diplomatic and commerical ties with Africa cut off. The existence of ties between Israel and South Africa, as well as Israeli conquest of Arab lands in 1967, also altered African relations toward Israel. Even the Ethiopian government, which had the strongest ties, had to agree to the African resolution at the 1973 OAU conference to condemn Israel and sever diplomatic ties. Nevertheless, covert Israeli-Ethiopian ties survived that resolution, and, as Moshe Dayan has inadvertently admitted, remain intact today.

The Israeli question was at first a uniting factor in Arab politics, bringing together regimes with very different ideologies. But since Sadat's visit to Jerusalem and the Camp David accords, the Arab world has been divided, with Egypt, somewhat timorously supported by the Sudan, prepared to negotiate a settlement with Israel under conditions unacceptable to most of the rest of the Arab world. As noted in the previous chapter, Saudi Arabia's reluctance to go along with Sadat was related more to its fear of being destabilized by the reconciled radical neighbors, Iraq and Syria, than to its insistence on the return of Jerusalem and the right of the Palestinians for self-determination. Nevertheless, the Saudis have consistently affirmed that peace in the Middle East can only come about if Israel withdraws its troops from the occupied territories and allows the Palestinians to determine their own future.

The fourth concern is Arab nationalism. This often takes the form of a claim that both the Somalis and the Eritreans are Arabs, and that their revolution is an extension of the "Arab revolution," usually meaning Baathist socialism, with its strong pan-Arab overtones. Fred Halliday, who defines an Arab as any person whose native language is Arabic, points out that the

Saudis emphasize the "Muslim" character of "those forces"—referring to the people of Eritrea and Somalia—while the Arab press often describes them as Arabs.

> For example, the Saudis have aided Muslim as against Christian elements within the Eritrean movement, and their overtures to Somalia have been couched in Islamic as much as Arab terms. The Iraqis, for their part, present the people in the area as part of the Arab national liberation struggle, and Baghdad's support is seen as part of Iraq's self-proclaimed pan-Arab anti-imperialist role.[3]

Halliday points out that the Arab states have used the question of Eritrea, as they have Palestine, to bolster their diplomatic position and win popularity at home. He adds that, as with the Palestinians, they have deployed money and weapons to manipulate dissension inside the Eritrean movement:

> The Saudis have been alarmed at the socialist orientation of the EPLF, and there is no doubt that a socialist independent Eritrea would be unwelcome to the conservative Arab states. Hence, whilst there is an Arab interest in Eritrea, it is less substantial and less consistent than either the Arab states or the Ethiopian government would have us believe.[4]

The fact that Arab governments have used the Eritrean struggle to win popularity at home suggests their awareness of the support of the Arab peoples for the Eritrean struggle. This is nowhere more true than in the Sudan, where the support of the great mass of Sudanese people has been a constant factor in the face of vacillating official policy. Later in this chapter I will discuss the best organized political force representing the masses in Sudanese politics—the Sudanese Communist Party—and its position on the struggle in the Horn. Because of its role in Sudanese political and social progress, and the prestige that it has acquired as a result, this party is the most important non-official political group in Sudanese politics. The positions it takes on such issues as the conflict in the Horn therefore carry a great deal of weight among influential sectors of Sudanese society. For this reason, I will discuss it at some length. First, however, more needs to be said about the role of Egypt and the Sudan in the region.

**Egypt and the Sudan**

An Ethiopian wit was once asked what Ethiopia's main export was. "Water," he answered, "water and the rich soil that goes with it." The Nile valley is the geographic link between Egypt and Ethiopia, and Egyptian rulers from ancient times have sought to control the river's source. Conversely, early Axumite rulers have extended their empire as far as Nubia in the upper Sudan, and at least one Abyssinian king contemplated diverting the course of the river in retaliation for Egypt's treatment of the Coptic Christians.[5]

The opening of the Suez Canal spurred another Egyptian territorial ambition, the desire to control the Bab el Mandeb at the mouth of the Red Sea. This failed, and it was not until the rise of Gamal Abdel Nasser that it was resumed. Nasser, however, attempted to legitimize his aim by cloaking it in an ideology of pan-Islam and pan-Arab socialism, augmented by pan-Africanism.

Nasser's pan-Arab socialism, with Egypt as the center, predominated during at least ten years of his rule. The pan-Islamic aspect was not exercised with any vigor, since it contradicted some of the secular aspects of socialist doctrine (Nasser's harsh treatment of the Ahwan Al Muslimin—the Muslim Brothers—is a manifestation of that contradiction), but it served a useful purpose in its appeal to Muslims of the world and of the region. In the Horn, the strength of this appeal was evident in May 1963, when Nasser came to Addis Ababa to attend the first OAU conference. Hundreds of thousands of Ethiopian Muslims spontaneously traveled (many on foot) to the airport to welcome him, completely surprising the Ethiopian authorities, who had very little way of gauging people's sentiments. The thunderous cry of "Nasser! Nasser!" still rings in the ears of many a member of the Ethiopian police and military. And the message was not lost on either the Ethiopian government or discerning observers.

How did this affect Nasser's African posture? By that time, his pan-Arab adventures had run into obstacles: first there was the failure of the United Arab Republic, where local sentiment was more than an as yet unclarified Arab socialist union could overcome. It ended when Syria withdrew from the union. Then came the intervention in North Yemen, to which Nasser committed over 25,000 Egyptian troops, in an inconclusive and costly struggle that had serious repercussions in domestic politics.

Nasser's adaptation to the emerging spirit of pan-Africanism, his contribution to the founding of the OAU, reveals the complex nature of Egyptian politics. In his view, Egyptians are Arabs, Muslims, and Africans, and they alone know in what order; this set of overlapping allegiances gives them an edge over others, but at the same time it may engender split loyalties that may make them a little suspect.

One of the curious and probably unintended consequences of the establishment of the OAU was that it formally imposed additional restraints on Nasser's ambition to be a regional power in the area, and particularly in the Horn. This reduced the pressure on the reactionary regimes in the region, including that of Haile Selassie. It therefore turned out, quite fortuitously as far as the Ethiopian government was concerned, to be a diplomatic triumph for the emperor. Further, the emperor and his successors have been able to use the OAU as a forum for bringing pressure to bear on any African country or movement with revolutionary intentions.

At the second OAU conference, held in Cairo in 1964 with Nasser presiding, a seal of legitimacy was placed on the colonially determined African borders. This further affected Nasser's ability to support liberation causes in the Horn, and the 1967 Arab-Israel war took care of the rest—although in fact, overt Egyptian support for the Eritrean cause had ceased long before 1967.

Meanwhile, the swift, bloodless *coup d'état* of military officers as a method of political change, which we may call the Nasserite model, was emulated across Africa, including in the Horn. It presented a nightmare to civilian governments and an opportunity for ambitious military officers. The first attempted coup occurred in Ethiopia in December 1960 and was led by Mengistu Neway, the leader of Haile Selassie's bodyguard. It misfired, in part because it was not carefully planned and in part because the emperor's unpopularity was limited to a narrowly based urban intelligentsia. Next came Nemeiry's coup in the Sudan in

May 1969, followed by Siad Barre's coup in Somalia in October. Both were successful and both were modelled on the Nasserite coup.[6] But whereas Siad steadily moved to the left, finally embracing and attempting to practice scientific socialism, Nemeiry followed the classic Nasserite line, as we shall see.

Sadat's policy toward Egyptian involvement in the Horn began to change in the aftermath of the 1973 Arab-Israeli war, when Kissinger's policy of gradual disengagement of both Egyptian and Israeli troops from the Sinai led Sadat to move toward a rapprochement with Israel—culminating in the Camp David accords. The expected result—ardently desired by Kissinger— was the abrogation of the Soviet-Egyptian friendship treaty in 1976. The Soviet Union thereupon intensified its presence in Somalia.

Reports of this alarmed the Sudanese and Egyptians, as well as the Saudis. When the Somalis failed to convince the Soviets to support them in the Ogaden, the convergence of interests, encouraged by Saudi promises of limitless cash, extended into the now embattled Somali capital. But when the moment of truth arrived, cash proved to be inadequate and was not matched by troops, Egyptian or otherwise.

Egypt and the Sudan, sharing a sense of insecurity, signed a mutual defense pact. Sadat left no room for doubt as to his hostility to the Soviet Union, when he stated on May 25, 1977:

> It is the desire of certain states to try to establish military bases in some of our states, exploiting disputes left over among us from previous regimes, and tempting us with arms, on the pretext of confronting the ambitions of neighboring countries. This will involve us in the struggle among the big powers and threaten us, our safety and security, as well as our freedom and independence. . . . Egypt wishes to draw the attention of all African people and states to this plot which is aimed at returning them to super power spheres of influence which service the economic interests and political and military considerations of those super powers.[7]

Nemeiry put it even more bluntly:

> I would like to draw the attention of African countries which have relations with these social neo-colonialists who enter Africa by flaunting the banner of supporting developing countries and

liberation movements. Be careful not to fall into their trap. I
sincerely advise you. My advice comes from our experience.[8]

The Soviet switch from Somalia to Ethiopia has brought the
sense of danger closer for Nemeiry. Relations between Ethiopia
and the Sudan have been periodically strained since the Sudan
gained its independence from British rule in 1956, and there has
in the past been armed conflict, including a major war in the
nineteenth century. The roots of conflict lie in the revolt of
southern Sudan against the central government in Khartoum,
and in the Eritrean liberation struggle. In the Sudan, Ethiopia
charged that the Sudan was helping Eritreans and the Sudanese
countered by claiming that the Ethiopians were helping the
revolt of the Anya Nya, an organization of predominantly Nilotic
people, most of whose leaders had been educated in Christian
mission schools. The Anya Nya felt an Arabization and Islamiza-
tion policy was being forced on them by the predominantly
Arabic-speaking central and northern Sudanese, who dominated
the government. Their claim for self-determination eventually
assumed a larger political perspective, transcending religion
and ethnic (or racial) factors, and gaining them the assistance of
European and U.S. Christians and the Ethiopian government.
The revolt ended in 1971, when Haile Selassie mediated a peace
agreement that provided for limited internal autonomy for the
southern Sudanese.

From that point on, Haile Selassie repeatedly encouraged
Nemeiry to press the Eritreans to settle in a similar fashion,
and no Sudanese government has ever officially supported the
Eritrean struggle. When Saddik el Mahdi was prime minister,
his government clamped down on the Eritreans, closing transit
and other facilities. Nemeiry somewhat relaxed these restric-
tions, but officially denied that he had done so. The only issue he
has openly and consistently raised is the question of the Eritrean
refugees who have lived in the Sudan since 1967; they are
estimated to number around 300,000, and mostly live in and
around refugee camps in border areas.

With the increase of Soviet influence in Ethiopia, Nemeiry's
policy has shifted toward a more open advocacy of the Eritreans'
right to self-determination. At the same time, he is anxious to

avoid a Soviet-backed Ethiopian incursion into his territory that might topple his regime, and he has shown a greater eagerness for conciliation than has Mengistu. The Khartoum meeting of the OAU in July 1978 adopted a report, by a committee that had been set up to mediate between the Sudan and Ethiopia, that described the "Eritrean conflict" as the main reason for bad relations between the two countries. As a follow-up, President Siaka Stevens of Sierra Leone convened a conciliation meeting in Freetown in February 1979, and Nemeiry put Eritrea at the top of the agenda. Mengistu then stated that there was no Eritrean problem, which terminated conciliation efforts. Recently, however, Mengistu appears to have become less arrogant and more conciliatory. He sent a delegation to attend the third congress of the Sudanese Socialist Union in January 1980, along with a special message and a piece of handicraft for Nemeiry. The shift reflects Mengistu's anxiety over Eritrea, and perhaps also events in Afghanistan, which show what happens when a nationalist leader is disliked by the Soviet leadership. There are now signs, following the failure of the Ethiopian military offensive in Eritrea, that Mengistu has become less intransigent, if only to gain time. Messages have been carried back and forth between Mengistu and Nemeiry, and there have been some overtures toward better bilateral relations.

Why does Nemeiry feel more threatened than Mengistu? Two critical events in Nemeiry's career explain his political behavior, including his sense of insecurity. First, there was an attempted coup in 1970 which allegedly involved a number of leading members of the Sudanese Communist Party, many of whom were later executed, including the distinguished Communist leader Abdel Khalig Mahgoub—an event which shocked the Sudanese population. Good relations between Sudan and the Soviet Union were threatened, but Nemeiry managed to smooth things over. The Sudanese left, including members of the now banned Communist Party, were less quick to forgive Nemeiry for either the executions or the ban imposed on their party, and were disappointed at the apparent betrayal of the Soviet Union. They had expected an emphatic denunciation, even a cutting of diplomatic ties. Instead, some members of the left felt that the Soviet Union made a deal with Nemeiry out of strategic considerations. The left in general, and the Sudanese Communist Party in particular, was a casualty.

The second event that explains Nemeiry's political behavior involved the Sudanese rightist movement, which was centered around Saddik el Mahdi, one-time prime minister, leader of the Umma Party, and great-grandson of the first Mahdi, and Sherif el Hindi, leader of the Unionist Party. These two men had been living in exile since Nemeiry's takeover, and Saddik was the central figure leading the opposition to his regime. Both Saddik and Sherif were charged with engineering an attempted coup in July 1976 and were tried in absentia. The charge included a reference to assistance originating from Libya and to the training of insurgents in Ethiopia. The coup had failed because Nemeiry's plane, which was to be the target of a mortar attack by units of the insurgent army, arrived an hour early, which foiled the attempt. Several hundred people were summarily tried and executed, and more were jailed. Sudanese sentiment was once again outraged at the number of executions. Nemeiry sensed this, and cleverly exploited anti-foreign as well as anti-reactionary feelings. The slogans carried by the demonstrators organized by his Sudanese Socialist Union in all the main urban centers reflected this tactic. One banner, for instance, read: "Lam Ta'udi Ya Raj' iya!"—"Oh Reaction! You shall never return!"

The result of the attempted coup was increasingly close relations between Egypt and the Sudan, and increasingly strained relations between them and Libya. A side effect was a change in Libyan support for the Eritrean struggle, from active espousal and considerable assistance to lukewarm tolerance and then a cessation of assistance altogether. Another consequence was the ironic fact that Cuban, Israeli, Libyan, and Yemeni officers were made to wait upon Mengistu, often all together at Menelik's palace.

While the Libyans have not actually denounced the Eritrean struggle, their financial support of Mengistu's regime has indirectly hurt a cause they had wholeheartedly supported for many years. A favorite remark of Ethiopian officials who tour Arab countries is that there are more Muslims in Ethiopia than in

Eritrea. Libya's Khadafi was impressed by this remark in late 1974, when he met the first delegation of the Dergue.[9]

The Libyan-backed attempted coup of July 1976 precipitated an Egypt-Sudan defense pact, which was aimed as much against Libya's penchant for intervention as against a possible "Communist" takeover in the Sudan. Fear of the former has grown with the massive influx of Soviet arms into Libya since 1975, and with Khadafi's open challenge to Sadat, which even led briefly to armed conflict between the two countries in July 1977. Fear of the latter grew out of the events in Ethiopia that climaxed with the Ogaden war.

The most important consequence of the Ogaden war for the Sudan has been the massive infusion of Soviet arms into Ethiopia and the consolidation of Mengistu's regime. Nemeiry's policy on Eritrea has been low-keyed mediation aimed at a resolution of the conflict in a manner similar to that in the southern Sudan. In January 1977, however, he openly declared his support for the Eritrean struggle. This came after the Arab states had taken the toughest stand ever in support of the Eritrean cause, and at a time when the Eritrean liberation fronts were winning battle after battle.

Nemeiry's stand shifted back to conciliation after he was elected chairman of the OAU in July 1978. The fear of Mengistu is as great as ever—and has become even greater since the Soviet-planned counteroffensive in Eritrea. On the other hand, Sudanese support for the Eritrean cause, including among members of Nemeiry's government, is too deep-rooted to accept any "deal" that might adversely affect the Eritrean struggle.

## The Role of the Sudanese Communist Party

The Sudanese Communist Party is one of the oldest—and, until its decimation, the best organized—parties in Africa or the Middle East. Its advent marked a crucial stage in the history of the region, and its development is a testimonial to the quality of its leadership and its program. Its disarray is linked both to

Nemeiry's cooptation of the progressive army officers and to the failure of the party's *"coup d'état."*

The Sudanese Communists' interest in the military officers and in the revolutionary potential of the army in general came after the Egyptian *coup d'état* in 1952. Abdel Khalig Mahgoub, secretary-general of the party, has summed up its views on this question.

> There is a necessary and close relationship between the army and the central question of every revolution, namely, that of state power. After the spontaneous upsurge of the masses is organized under the leadership of the revolutionary party, revolution triumphs when the army is either no longer capable of suppressing the revolutionary movement or unwilling to defend the old regime, effective sections of it having sided with the revolution. This makes it imperative that we define our attitude toward the armed forces in our country.
>
> Our point of departure is the nature, tasks, and social forces of the national democratic revolution. Guided by this scientific class approach, we give prominence in our work to building the permanent alliance between the working class and the peasantry, as the backbone of the alliance of all the national democratic forces. Addressing ourselves to these forces within the army, especially to the soldiers, the majority of whom come from the rural areas, we call on them to join the alliance.
>
> The fundamental issue in our tactics is to organize the national democratic classes and states, to build their alliance under the leadership of the working class, and to bring their activity to its highest level, i.e., to revolution. Consequently, we reject the erroneous view which holds that work among the democratic elements in the army should come first in our party's activity, on the ground that, having access to arms, they are more capable of settling the question of power swiftly and decisively. In essence, such views are putschist; they lead the party to the renunciation of work among the masses and convert it into a conspiratorial group seeking change through coups d'état.[10]

It is difficult to believe that a man who wrote such a piece, a man with Mahgoub's lucidity and learning, could have been actively involved in the 1970 attempted coup. His surviving comrades certainly do not believe he was. He has since become a martyr, and his words have become points of reference, along with those of Marx and Lenin. The party central committee concludes its remarks with the assertion that "coup tactics, in as much as they are endorsed by the national democratic forces, correspond to the interests of the national and petty bourgeoisie. For the Communist Party there is no alternative to mass action."

Referring to events in Ethiopia since the spring of 1974, the central committee attempts to distinguish the Portuguese and Ethiopian coups from "traditional" coups. In traditional coups the officers monopolize decision-making, whereas the Portuguese and Ethiopian coups "were characterized by the breadth of the base which took part in the preparatory work . . . and the prevalence of soldiers and noncoms taking part in planning and execution." Although in the Ethiopian case, this was true only in the initial stages, the main point to emphasize is the striking parallel between the Portuguese and Ethiopian revolutions, because in both cases colonial wars played a crucial role in bringing down the old regime. To paraphrase Samora Machel, both the Portuguese and the Ethiopians have had the armed forces topple autocratic and unpopular regimes, but they could not be revolutionary and colonialist at the same time. But the parallel ends here, because while the Portuguese listened and then hastened the end of Portuguese colonial rule, the Dergue has refused to reply in kind. As the central committee concluded: "The forward march of the revolutionary process in Ethiopia demands that the coup no longer remain a coup—i.e., that it become a deep revolutionary movement. The principal and the first condition for such development is the institution of democracy." Unfortunately, the Ethiopian revolution has been progressing in the opposite direction, with tragic consequence.

In its concern to spare the Ethiopian revolution from the blight of reaction and imperialist control, the Sudanese Communist Party has called upon all progressive forces in the region to take steps to strengthen and develop "the broadest forms of mass political struggle of the peoples of our region to roll back the onslaught of U.S.A. and the Ryadh-Cairo axis and to defend the revolutionary positions and organizations of our peoples." It has also called upon Ethiopia, Somalia, and Eritrea to seek a democratic solution to their problems.

The pursuit of such goals is based on certain principles, including the need for a democratic revolution in Ethiopia, and recognition of the right of the Eritreans and other peoples in the former Ethiopian empire to self-determination.

Elsewhere in the document there are appeals to the democratic process as the solution to political problems in the Sudan itself. The conciliation efforts between Nemeiry and the Umma and Unionist party leaders are analyzed as the result of a neo-colonial conspiracy to consolidate and expand their position in the Sudan and in the region.

Alas, events in 1978 made short work of their appeals for a democratic solution in either the Ethiopian-Somali conflict or in the Eritrean struggle. Differences between the Sudanese Communist Party and the Communist Party of the Soviet Union, whose relations have in the past been extremely cordial, turn on disagreement about the role of democratic revolutionaries—since the Soviet Union's "noncapitalist development" model eschews the national democratic revolution. The document appears to deal with the Soviet Union's attempt to force a military (and therefore nondemocratic) solution in Eritrea by referring to Marxism-Leninism as the common theory and heritage of all communist and workers' parties and then stating: "They are all duty-bound to develop it and simultaneously to defend it against danger from any quarter whatever. Hence the need to draw the line between the right of every party to formulate its own tactics and the right of any other party to conclude that these tactics represent a certain departure from Marxism-Leninism."

Experience shows, the paragraph goes on, that there is a material basis for the emergence of opportunist trends that cross the borders of their native lands. In such cases the common struggle against them becomes an internationalist obligation. A practical formula is clearly needed for the fraternal exchange of views, and for developing the concepts of internationalism and independence so that they complement rather than contradict each other. The central committee appears, however, to be anxious to see that the differences with the Soviet party do not impair cooperation and solidarity between them, and states: "We adhere strictly to this attitude, despite the severe tests to which it was and is being put."

Events in the Horn have been running ahead of the ideological position taken by the leadership of the Sudanese Communist Party. There is a historic link between the Sudanese Communist Party and the Communist Party of the Soviet Union, marked mostly by high esteem, cordiality, and understanding. But differences have emerged on at least two points. The first and most important, and the one most relevant to the present discussion, concerns the Soviet Union's military involvement on the side of the Dergue against the Eritrean struggle. The Sudanese Communist Party supports the right of the Eritrean people to self-determination, and thus by implication condemns the Soviet reversal of policy on this issue. A further difference concerns the Sovet Union's "non-capitalist" model of development, which is rejected by the Sudanese Communist Party in favor of a national democratic program—thus bringing it closer to the EPLF. The implications of these differences need to be properly grasped if future events are to be understood.

# 8

## Summary and Conclusion

The conflict in the Horn of Africa involves five interrelated elements: (1) The reality of the Ethiopian empire, and the imperial question it poses; (2) the national question, which is the antithesis of the imperial question; (3) the Eritrean war of liberation, and the colonial question it raises; (4) the Ethiopian-Somali conflict, stemming from the Ogaden (Western Somalia) question; and (5) the involvement of foreign powers, including military intervention.

### The Imperial and National Questions

The principal source of the Horn's conflict is the Ethiopian state, whose imperial character persisted after the overthrow of Haile Selassie's semi-feudal regime in 1974. The persistence of the imperial question has inevitably raised the national question, since the two are dialectically connected. Haile Selassie's feudal empire was built by conquest and the subjugation of many nations by the ruling Amhara nation. This entailed oppression and exploitation, of human and material resources, as a feudal land tenure system was imposed on the conquered peoples. Feudalism thus combined with imperial conquest to produce the Ethiopian empire-state. It was therefore expected that the emperor's overthrow and the subsequent abolition of the

166

feudal land tenure system would be accompanied by the transformation of the imperial state, bringing with it a new basis of
consent and of equality among the various nations comprising
the empire. Yet contrary to expectations, and to repeated demands, the new rulers have shown no principled commitment
to any such new basis of consent and equality, and certainly not
to the principle of self-determination, despite rhetoric to the
contrary. In fact, no sooner did the military regime consolidate
itself in power than it began to send expeditionary forces to
suppress national movements, most notably those among the
Oromo and in Tigray. The failed expectations, the unmet demands,
and the acts of supression drove countless Oromo and Tigrean
cadre to join their respective liberation fronts, often after hesitation and sometimes after initially supporting the Dergue.

Allied to the national question is the democratic question, for
the crisis of empire is reflected in the way the democratic question has been handled. The revolutionary upsurge that engulfed
Ethiopia in the spring of 1974 was manifestly popular, though it
had no organized leadership. The state of disarray of the democratic and progressive forces in the 1974–1977 period was proof
of the lack of unity and invited the dominant role of the military,
which played one faction off against the other and eventually
succeeded in imposing a military dictatorship with only the
outward trappings of progress. Before the fratricidal wars between the EPRP and MEISON came to a close, it was proposed to
begin a democratic dialogue between all progressive forces, in
order to form a united front against the common enemy—the
remnants of feudalism, bureaucratic capitalism, imperialism,
and all the forces of reaction. A faction within the Dergue
was even persuaded of the necessity, and correctness, of such
a dialogue. Yet the idea was rejected and all its proponents
liquidated, together with those left in the EPRP and MEISON.
All this reflected the ascendancy within the Dergue of an autocratic, anti-democratic military group that fears democratic and
national forces equally. It has been one of the contentions of this
book that a military establishment that was a faithful servant of
the feudo-imperial state, and whose members were steeped in
feudal values, could not be expected to shed those legacies

easily. Hence the fear and suspicion of all democratic forces; hence also the failure of the revolution.

## The Eritrean War of Liberation

In the same way that a transformation of the empire would have resolved the national question, so it would have opened the way to a solution of the colonial question in Eritrea. Modern Eritrea was forged as an Italian colony at the same time that Menelik's expansion through conquest was forging the Ethiopian empire-state. An Ethiopia reconstructed on a new basis of consent would have facilitated the resolution of the Eritrean war, as some Eritreans—including the writer—hoped, being equally sanguine about the democratic course of the Ethiopian revolution. In this, too, events denied hopes. When Aman Andom was killed because of his insistence on a negotiated settlement of the Eritrean war, Mengistu's faction insisted on a military solution. The result was an escalation of the war, and this in turn confirmed the Eritrean freedom fighters in the necessity of armed struggle, and expanded their influence by leaps and bounds.

Meanwhile, the Eritrean national liberation struggle had become a revolutionary force that brought about radical social reconstruction. The EPLF not only met the awesome challenge of a much greater Ethiopian army, but it galvanized the Eritrean nation, organizing, politicizing, and arming the people. The Dergue's response to military defeat was to increase its military involvement, which has driven it deeper into debt and into dependence on the Soviet Union. Backed to the hilt by Soviet arms and advised by Soviet officers at strategic as well as tactical (combat) levels, the Dergue launched what it proclaimed as a final crushing blow in the spring of 1978. After initial successes, the 120,000-strong army of invasion once again suffered defeat at the hands of the EPLF guerrilla army—which followed up with a counteroffensive of its own, begun in December 1979. This has had serious repercussions within the Dergue's army, including summary executions of officers and soldiers critical of the campaign. It has also demonstrated once again that superiority in numbers and arms is not enough to defeat a popular war waged for a just cause and embraced by an organized and politicized nation.

Yet the Dergue refuses to give up the military solution, and the suffering continues. The Ethiopian economy is held hostage to the war, and the course of the once-popular revolution has been diverted. The Eritreans, for their part, have girded themselves for a protracted struggle, confident of eventual victory.

### The Ethiopian-Somali Conflict and the Ogaden (Western Somalia)

The conflict between Ethiopia and Somalia over the Ogaden question reflects one aspect of the failure of the post-colonial African legal order. Somalia, a member of the OAU, has from its birth as an independent nation in 1960 claimed the Ogaden, which it calls Western Somalia, on the basis of a historic unity and of the uninterrupted struggle of the people of the area against alien occupiers—including Ethiopians, British, and Italians. This has meant that the Ogaden should have been decolonized with the rest of the colonial territories. Somali demands to that effect were not accepted by the OAU at its founding conference in Addis Ababa in May 1963, or at its second meeting in Cairo in July 1964. It has been argued above that one of the major reasons was the way in which Haile Selassie was able to use the image of a Pandora's box to foreclose further debate on colonial boundaries.

Yet this solution failed to deal with the issue of self-determination for a people trapped within the colonial inherited boundaries, a people who nevertheless make good their claim by waging an armed struggle. And with the failure of diplomacy, Somalia has become more vigorous in its aid of the people of the Ogaden, and commenced active military involvement in 1977 when the Soviet Union decided to side with the Dergue. With the short-lived Ogaden war of 1977–1978, the conflict was internationalized.

**Foreign Involvement**

The reversal of alliances that brought Soviet military might to the rescue of the Dergue in 1977 has turned events in the Horn in unexpected directions, forestalling their early resolution. But outside involvement did not begin in 1977: in the 1950s the United States signed a defense pact with Haile Selassie, thus stepping into the shoes of the European colonial powers in the region. This alliance obviously entailed support of the Ethiopian empire-state and of Haile Selassie's imperial ambitions in Eritrea. The Soviet Union, on the other hand, openly supported the Eritrean people's demand for independence, and directly or indirectly encouraged national movements aimed at the heart of the empire-state.

The Soviet reversal, from support of the Eritrean cause to support of the Dergue, following on its intervention in the Ogaden, also implies acceptance of the empire-state and a denial of the principle of self-determination. The Soviet Union has thus put its national interest above principle and above solidarity with a just cause, and has exported arms to advance this interest. Whether the Soviet military involvement in Ethiopia can be translated into a permanent political and socioeconomic presence will depend on the outcome of the many aspects of the conflict in the area, including within Ethiopia itself. The difference between the Soviet and Western presences is that whereas the former places heavy reliance on arms, as the thin end of the wedge, the latter (and especially the United States) is relying on historically rooted economic interests and the capitalist world market, into which the region's economy has been integrated.

The Dergue knows this and tries to make the best of both worlds—Soviet arms and Western money, including U.S. and EEC economic aid. Yet the failure of the military campaign in Eritrea, and the continuation of the guerrilla war in the Ogaden, must surely cause the Soviet Union to begin to question the efficacy of weapons-peddling as the instrument of a national strategic policy. On the other hand, since a victory for the Dergue would mean less need to rely on the Soviet military presence, the failure of the campaign and the continued guerrilla war should not be much regreted by Soviet strategists in the present circumstances. Eventually, the events in Afghanistan and the intractable nature of the national question in the Horn may chasten them, as the West sits tight and expends comparatively fewer resources while reaping the harvest of Soviet failure. The prospect of such an eventuality should be enough to cause a reappraisal of Soviet policy, one element of which would be a proper understanding of the national question in Ethiopia and a reversion to supporting the Eritrean cause.

In the short run, then, the Horn of Africa seems destined only for more conflict. Weapons will keep pouring in and influence-peddling will continue. The OAU, which is in principle opposed to outside control of the destiny of any part of Africa, is too weak and too divided to put a stop to such intervention.

Ultimately, however, the Ethiopian empire must be transformed. The most likely cause will be the success of the Eritrean freedom fighters, for a final failure of the Ethiopian military campaign will mean the same end for the Dergue that it did for Haile Selassie. The wars of liberation in Tigray, in the Ogaden, and among the Oromo will also contribute to the empire's fall. If and when all this happens, there will be a new basis for a reconstructed Ethiopia. That, together with an independent Eritrea and a friendly Somalia, could change the crisis of empire into a triumph of the people of the Horn. They may then, if they so choose, unite to build the region on a popular, progressive, and anti-imperialist foundation. That would indeed be an inspiration to the rest of the continent.

# Appendices

# Appendix 1
# Speech of the Soviet Delegate to the United Nations

The USSR delegation would like to explain its vote on the various draft resolutions. Three draft resolutions have been submitted to the General Assembly on the question of Eritrea: a draft resolution submitted by the Soviet Union (A/1570), providing that Eritrea should be granted independence immediately, a draft resolution submitted by Poland (A/1564 and Corr. 1), providing that Eritrea should be granted independence after three years, and a draft resolution submitted by the Ad Hoc Political Committee, providing that Eritrea should be federated with Ethiopia.

The USSR has consistently supported the proposal that Eritrea should be granted independence and has continued to do so at the current session. We base our argument on the fact that all peoples have a right to self-determination and national independence.

The national liberation struggle of the colonial and independent peoples for their independence and freedom has grown in strength as a result of the Second World War. The colonial system is going through an acute crisis. Accordingly, in considering the fate of Eritrea—one of the former Italian colonies—the United Nations must take a decision which will satisfy the longing of the Eritrean people for independence and freedom from national oppression. The General Assembly cannot tolerate a deal by the colonial powers at the expense of the population of Eritrea.

In the circumstances, the only solution to the problem of the future of Eritrea is to grant independence. And here it should be noted that the continuation of British administration for any period whatsoever would be fatal to the normal development of Eritrea.

The situation in Eritrea has considerably deteriorated during the period of British administration. Significant facts testifying to this are given in the report of the United Nations Commission for Eritrea, in the memorandum submitted by the delegations of Guatemala and Pakistan. In that memorandum the following conclusion is drawn from the examination and analysis of those facts: "During the last decade nothing has been done toward the economic improvement of the territory, whereas much has been done to the contrary," that is to say, toward worsening the situation.

Eritrea must not be left for any further period under the administration of the United Kingdom, which is pursuing a policy clearly designed to worsen the situation in Eritrea. Any further deterioration of the situation in Eritrea can be prevented by the immediate grant of independence, which a large part of the population of Eritrea itself is demanding. The memorandum to which I have already referred states that: "The great majority of the eastern and western lowlands, and groups of varying importance in the plateau, were in favor of immediate independence."

The arguments used against the proposal that Eritrea should be granted immediate independence are those habitually adduced in defense of the colonial system. It is alleged, for instance, that Eritrea is a backward country and is not ready for independence, that an independent Eritrea would not be able to ensure its own independent economic development, and, as the United Kingdom representative said at the meetings of the Ad Hoc Political Committee, that to grant independence to Eritrea would lead to political chaos. Thus we see that the usual arguments which are advanced to defend the colonial system are being used here.

I know of no single instance in history where a colonial country has won its independence without being confronted by the allegation that it was not ready for independence.

The General Assembly cannot attach importance to arguments of this kind. On the contrary, it should reject them once and for all, and decide to grant Eritrea independence immediately. Furthermore, the British occupation forces should be withdrawn three months from the day on which the General Assembly decision to grant Eritrea independence is adopted. The continued retention of United Kingdom occupation forces in Eritrea is absolutely unjustified, and is incompatible both with the national interests of Eritrea itself and with the fundamental principles and purposes of the United Nations.

It is clear from the foregoing that the USSR delegation objects to the proposal for the federation of Eritrea with another state, as such a federation would disregard the right of the Eritrean people to self-determination by preventing the Eritreans from exercising that right. The delegation of the Soviet Union bases its position on the fact that such a decision is being imposed on the Eritrean people without their consent and, hence, in violation of the fundamental principle of the right of self-determination of people.

A number of speakers here have referred to federation as a compromise solution. The USSR delegation considers that if federation is indeed a compromise solution, it represents a compromise among the colonial powers. It is being imposed on the Eritrean people and, in effect, on Ethiopia also, and it will be equally unsatisfactory to Ethiopia.

In reality, this solution is not the kind of compromise which should be proposed by the General Assembly. In the first place, how can one speak of a compromise if it has been adopted without the participation of the peoples concerned, that is, without the participation of Eritrea? Furthermore, it has been adopted, notwithstanding the Eritrean people's wishes, against their interests and in violation of their most vital, fundamental right—the right of self-determination.

Federation cannot therefore be called a compromise solution. In reality, it is the outcome of the contest among the colonial powers for a new partition of the former Italian colonies.

We are told that a part of the population of Eritrea desires federation. Even if that were so, the question should be decided by the Eritrean people themselves, and not by some international organization. In any case, it cannot be settled by an agreement among the colonial powers. The federal solution has in fact been put forward by the colonial powers, under the guidance of the United States.

The idea of federation was submitted by the United States at the last session of the General Assembly. That fact in itself proves that the problem is not now being settled in the interests of the Eritrean people. In recent times, the United States has become the dominating power in Africa, and determines the colonial policy of the various states in that continent.

This is what an American newspaper says about the colonial interests of the United States in Africa. The *Sunday Compass* of 19 November 1950 says: "Though it possesses no colonies in Africa, the United States is today the dominant power in Africa. And it is using its power, not to promote the support of anti-colonialism in Africa, but to strengthen and extend the old colonial pattern. Such changes as it has brought about are changes which divert profits from London and Paris to New York."

Thus the United States has become the dominant power which directs the colonial subjugation and exploitation of the African peoples and the proposal for federation, which was put foward by the United States delegation, reflects the interests of the colonial powers, headed by the United States.

The USSR delegation cannot therefore support the proposal for federation, which is the outcome of the struggle among the colonial powers for a new partition of the former Italian colonies.

The USSR delegation appeals to all the other delegations to vote in favor of Eritrean independence, which is the equitable solution to this problem. An independent Eritrea would have the right to decide all questions concerning its relations with neighboring states.

In the light of all these considerations, the USSR delegation continues to urge that a decision should be taken to grant Eritrea immediate independence, to withdraw the British occupation troops from Eritrea within three months, and to give Ethiopia access to the sea through the port of Assab.

These are the principles by which the delegation of the Soviet Union will be guided in voting on the three draft resolutions submitted to us on the question of the future of Eritrea.

# Appendix 2
# Proclamation on the
# Establishment of the Dergue

Although the people of Ethiopia have looked, in good faith, upon the Crown as a symbol of their unity, Haile Selassie I, who has ruled the country for more than fifty years, ever since he assumed power as a Crown Prince, has abused the authority, dignity, and honor of office for the personal benefit and interest of himself, his immediate family, and retainers. As a consequence, he has led the country into its present inextricable situation. Moreover, as he has progressed in age, being eighty-two years old, he cannot shoulder the high responsibilities of his office.

The present parliamentary system is not democratic. The members of parliament have so far served not the nation but the ruling aristocratic class and themselves. Hence, the members of parliament have refrained from legislating on fundamental national matters such as land reform while legislating laws to promote their interests and that of their class, thereby adding to the misery of the people. The existence of this parliament is inimical to the philosophy and objectives of "Ethiopia Tikdem."

Likewise, the 1955 revised constitution was designed to give absolute power to the emperor while providing a democratic façade for the benefit of world public opinion. The constitution was not conceived to safeguard the rights of the people. In fact, the constitution abrogates the natural rights of man by decreeing that these rights were granted to the people by the emperor. As such, the 1955 constitution diametrically opposes the present popular movement for economic, political, and social reforms.

179

The feudal system of government has mismanaged the affairs of the country, leading it into the present economic, social, and political quagmire. Therefore, the following proclamation has been promulgated to establish a provisional administrative machinery for the transitional period and for the progress of the country and the security of the people.

1. This proclamation may be cited as the Provisional Military Government of Ethiopia Proclamation, No. 1/1967.

2. Haile Selassie I has been deposed as of today, Meskerem 2, 1967 (September 12, 1974).

3. a. The Crown Prince, His Highness Merid Azmatch Asfa Wossen, will become King of Ethiopia.
   b. The coronation ceremony will be held as soon as the Crown Prince returns to his country.
   c. The King will be head of state with no power in the country's administrative and political affairs.

4. Until the people elect their genuine representatives in truly democratic elections, Parliament (the Senate and Chamber of Deputies) has been closed down forthwith.

5. a. The revised constitution of 1955 is suspended.
   b. The new draft constitution, the promulgation of which has been demanded by the Armed Forces Committee as a matter of urgency, shall be put into effect after necessary improvements are made to include provisions reflecting the social, economic, and political philosophy of the new Ethiopia and to safeguard the civil rights of the people.

6. The Armed Forces Committee has assumed full government power until a legally constituted people's assembly approves a new constitution and a government is duly established.

7. All courts of law throughout the country shall continue their normal functions.

8. It is hereby prohibited, for the duration of this proclamation, to oppose the aims of the philosophy, "Ethiopia Tikdem," to engage in any strike, hold unauthorized demonstrations or public meetings, or to engage in any act that may disturb public peace and security.

9. A special military tribunal shall be established to try those

who contravene the orders enunciated in No. 8 of this proclamation and also to try former and present government officials who may be charged with corruption and abuse of power. Judgments handed down by the special military tribunal are not subject to appeal.

10. All existing laws that do not contravene the provisions of this proclamation and those of future orders shall remain in effect.

11. This proclamation shall be in force as of Meskerem 2, 1967 (September 12, 1974).

The Committee of the Armed Forces,
Police, and Territorial Army
Addis Ababa, September 12, 1974

# Appendix 3
# National Democratic Program
# of the Eritrean
# People's Liberation Front

### 1. Establish a People's Democratic State

A.  Abolish the Ethiopian colonial administrative organs and all anti-national and undemocratic laws, as well as nullify the military, economic, and political treaties affecting Eritrea signed between colonial Ethiopia and other governments.

B.  Safeguard the interests of the masses of workers, peasants, and other democratic forces.

C.  Set up a people's assembly, constituted of people's representatives democratically and freely elected from anti-feudal and anti-imperialist patriotic forces. The people's assembly shall draw the constitution, promulgate laws, elect the people's administration, and ratify national economic plans and new treaties.

D.  Protect the people's democratic rights—freedom of speech, the press, assembly, worship, and peaceful demonstration; develop anti-feudal and anti-imperialist worker, peasant, women, student, and youth organizations.

E.  Assure all Eritrean citizens equality before the law without distinction as to nationality, tribe, region, sex, cultural level, occupation, position, wealth, faith, etc.

F.  Severely punish Eritrean lackeys of Ethiopian colonialism who have committed crimes against the nation and the people.

### 2. Build an Independent, Self-Reliant, and Planned National Economy

A.  *Agriculture*

1.  Confiscate all land in the hands of the aggressor Ethiopian

regime, the imperialists, Zionists, and Eritrean lackeys and put it in the service of the Eritrean masses.

2. Make big nationalized farms and extensive farms requiring modern techniques state farms and use their produce for the benefit of the masses.

3. Abolish feudal land relations and carry out an equitable distribution of land. Strive to introduce cooperative farms by creating conditions of cooperation and mutual assistance so as to develop a modern and advanced system of agriculture and animal husbandry capable of increasing the income and improving the lot of the peasantry.

4. Induce the peasants to adopt modern agricultural techniques, introduce them to advanced agricultural implements and provide them with advisors, experts, veterinary services, fertilizers, wells, dams, transportation, finance, etc., in order to alleviate their problems and improve their livelihood and working conditions.

5. Provide the nomads with veterinary services, livestock breeding experts, agricultural advisors, and financial assistance in order to enable them to lead settled lives, adopt modern techniques of agriculture and animal husbandry, and improve their livelihood.

6. Provide for the peaceful and amicable settlement of land disputes and inequality among individuals and villages in such a way as to harmonize the interest of the aggrieved party with that of the national economic interest.

7. Advance the economic and living conditions in, and bridge the gap between, the cities and the countryside.

8. Make pastures and forests state property, preserve wild life and forestry, and fight soil erosion.

9. Maintain a proper balance between agriculture and industry in the context of the planned economy.

10. Promote an association that will organize, politicize, and arm the peasants with a clear revolutionary outlook so they can fully participate in the anti-colonial and anti-feudal struggle, defend the gains of the revolution, free themselves from oppression and economic exploitation, and manage their own affairs.

B. *Industry*

1.  Nationalize all industries in the hands of the imperialists, Zionists, Ethiopian colonialists, and their Eritrean lackeys, as well as resident aliens opposed to Eritrean independence.

2.  Nationalize big industries, ports, mines, public transport, communications, power plants, and other basic economic resources.

3.  Exploit marine resources, expand the production of salt and other minerals, develop the fish industry, explore for oil and other minerals.

4.  Allow nationals who were not opposed to the independence of Eritrea to participate in national construction by owning small factories and workshops compatible with national development and the system of administration.

5.  Strive to develop heavy industry so as to promote light industry, advance agriculture, and combat industrial dependence.

C. *Finance*

1.  Nationalize all insurance companies and banks, so as to centralize banking operations, regulate economic activities and accelerate economic development.

2.  Establish a government-owned central national bank and issue an independent national currency.

3.  Prohibit usury in all its forms and extend credit at the lowest interest in order to eliminate the attendant exploitation of the masses.

4.  Design and implement an appropriate tariff policy to secure the domestic market for the nation's agricultural, industrial, and handicraft products.

5.  Formulate and implement an equitable and rational taxation policy to administer and defend the country, carry out production and social functions.

D. *Trade*

1.  Construct essential land, air, and sea transportation and communications to develop the nation's trade.

2.  Handle all import and export trade.

3.  Nationalize the big trading companies and regulate the small ones.

4. Prohibit the export of essential commodities and limit the import of luxury goods.

5. Regulate the exchange and pricing of the various domestic products.

6. Strictly prohibit contraband trade.

7. Establish trade relations with all countries that respect Eritrean sovereignty irrespective of political systems.

E. *Urban Land and Housing*

1. Make urban land state property.

2. Nationalize all excess urban houses in order to abolish exploitation through rent and improve the livelihood of the masses.

3. Set, taking the standard of living into account, a rational rent price in order to improve the living conditions of the masses.

4. Compensate citizens for nationalized property in accordance with a procedure based on personal income and the condition of the national economy.

5. Build appropriate modern houses to alleviate the shortage of housing for the masses.

## 3. Develop Culture, Education, Technology, and Public Health

A. *Culture*

1. Obliterate the decadent culture and disgraceful social habits that Ethiopian colonialism, world imperialism, and Zionism have spread in order to subjugate and exploit the Eritrean people and destroy their identity.

2. In the new educational curriculum, provide for the proper dissemination, respect, and development of the history of Eritrea and its people, the struggle against colonialism, oppression, and for national independence, the experience, sacrifices, and heroism as well as the national folklore, traditions, and culture of the Eritrean people.

3. Destroy the bad aspects of the culture and traditions of Eritrean society and develop its good and progressive content.

4. Ensure that the Eritrean people glorify and eternally cherish the memory of the heroic martyrs of the struggle for independence who, guided by revolutionary principles, gave their lives for the salvation of their people and country.

B. *Education and Technology*

1. Combat illiteracy to free the Eritrean people from the darkness of ignorance.

2. Provide for universal compulsory education up to the middle school.

3. Establish institutions of higher education in the various fields of science, arts, technology, agriculture, etc.

4. Grant students scholarships to pursue studies in the various fields of learning.

5. Establish schools in the various regions of Eritrea in accordance with need.

6. Separate education from religion.

7. Make the state run all the schools and provide free education at all levels.

8. Integrate education with production and put it in the service of the masses.

9. Enable nationals, especially the students and youth, to train and develop themselves in the sciences, literature, handicrafts, and technology through the formation of their own organizations.

10. Provide favorable work conditions for experts and the skilled to enable them to utilize their skills and knowledge in the service of the masses.

11. Engage in educational, cultural, and technological exchange with other countries on the basis of mutual benefit and equality.

C. *Public Health*

1. Render medical services freely to the people.

2. Eradicate contagious diseases and promote public health by building the necessary hospitals and health centers all over Eritrea.

3. Scientifically develop traditional medicine.

4. Establish sports and athletic facilities and popularize them among the masses.

### 4. Safeguard Social Rights

A. *Workers' Rights*

1. Politicize and organize the workers, whose participation in the struggle has been hindered by the reactionary line and lead-

ership, and enable them, in a higher and more organized form, to play their vanguard role in the revolution.

2. Abolish the system of labor laws and sham trade unions set up by Ethiopian colonialism and its imperialist masters to oppress Eritrean workers.

3. Enforce an eight-hour working day and protect the right of workers to rest one day a week and twenty-five days a year.

4. Promulgate a special labor code that properly protects the rights of workers and enables them to form unions.

5. Assure workers comfortable housing and decent living conditions.

6. Devise a social security program to care for and assist workers who, because of illness, disability, or age, are unable to work.

7. Prohibit unjustified dismissals and undue pay cuts.

8. Protect the right of workers to participate in the management and administration of enterprises and industries.

9. Struggle to eliminate unemployment and protect every citizen's right to work.

B. *Women's Rights*

1. Develop an association through which women can participate in the struggle against colonial aggression and for social transformation.

2. Outline a broad program to free women from domestic confinement, develop their participation in social production, and raise their political, cultural, and technical levels.

3. Assure women full rights of equality with men in politics, economy, and social life, as well as equal pay for equal work.

4. Promulgate progressive marriage and family laws.

5. Protect the right of women workers to two months' maternity leave with full pay.

6. Protect the right of mothers and children, provide delivery, nursery, and kindergarten services.

7. Fight to eradicate prostitution.

8. Respect the right of women not to engage in work harmful to their health.

9. Design programs to increase the number and upgrade the quality of women leaders and public servants.

C. *Families of Martyrs, Disabled Fighters, and Others Need-ing Social Assistance*

1. Provide necessary care and assistance to all fighters and other citizens who, in the course of the struggle against Ethiopian colonialism and for national salvation, have suffered disability in jails or in armed combat.

2. Provide assistance and relief to the victims of Ethiopian colonial aggression, orphans, the old and the disabled, as well as those harmed by natural causes.

3. Render necessary assistance and care for the families of martyrs.

### 5. Insure the Equality and Consolidate the Unity of Nationalities

A. Abolish the system and laws instituted by imperialism, Ethiopian colonialism, and their lackeys in order to divide, oppress, and exploit the Eritrean people.

B. Rectify all errors committed by opportunists in the course of the struggle.

C. Combat national chauvinism as well as narrow nationalism.

D. Nurture and strengthen the unity and fraternity of Eritrean nationalities.

E. Accord all nationalities equal rights and responsibilities in leading them toward national progress and salvation.

F. Train cadre from nationalities in various fields to assure common progress.

G. Safeguard the right of all nationalities to preserve and develop their spoken or written language.

H. Safeguard the right of all nationalities to preserve and develop their progressive culture and traditions.

I. Forcefully oppose those who, in the pursuit of their own interests, create cliques on the basis of nationality, tribe, region, etc. and obstruct the unity of the revolution and the people.

### 6. Build a Strong People's Army

A. Liberate the land and the people step by step through the strategy of people's war. Build a strong land, air, and naval force capable of defending the country's borders, territorial waters, air space, and territorial integrity, as well as the full independence, progress, and dignity of its people in order to attain prosperity and reach the highest economic stage. The people's army shall be: politically conscious, imbued with comradely relations, steeled through revolutionary discipline; full of resoluteness, imbued with a spirit of self-sacrifice, participating in production; and equipped with modern tactics, weapons, and skills.

Being the defender of the interests of the workers and peasants, it serves the entire people of Eritrea irrespective of religion, nationality, or sex. The basis of this army is the revolutionary force presently fighting for national independence and liberation.

B. Establish a people's militia to safeguard the gains of the revolution and support the people's army in the liberated and semi-liberated areas.

C. Establish a progressive and advanced military academy.

### 7. Respect Freedom of Religion and Faith

A. Safeguard every citizen's freedom of religion and belief.

B. Completely separate religion from the state and politics.

C. Separate religion from education and allow no compulsory education.

D. Strictly oppose all the imperialist-created new counter-revolutionary faiths, such as Jehovah's Witnesses, Pentecostals, Bahai, etc.

E. Legally punish those who try to sow discord in the struggle and undermine the progress of the Eritrean people on the basis of religion, whether in the course of the armed struggle or in a people's democratic Eritrea.

### 8. Provide Humane Treatment to Prisoners of War and Encourage Desertion of Eritrean Soldiers Serving the Enemy

A. Oppose the efforts of Ethiopian colonialism to conscript duped soldiers to serve as tools of aggression for the oppression and slaughter of the Eritrean people.

B. Encourage Eritrean soldiers and plainclothesmen who have been duped into serving in the Ethiopian colonial army to return to the just cause and join their people in the struggle against Ethiopian aggression and welcome them to its ranks with full rights of equality.

C. Provide humane treatment and care for Ethiopian war prisoners.

D. Severely punish the die-hard, criminal, and atrocious henchmen and lackeys of Ethiopian colonialism.

## 9. Protect the Rights of Eritreans Residing Abroad

A. Struggle to organize Eritreans residing abroad in the already formed mass organization so they can participate in the patriotic anti-colonial struggle.

B. Strive to secure the rights of Eritrean refugees in the neighboring countries, win them the assistance of international organizations, and work for the improvement of their living conditions.

C. Welcome nationals who want to return to their country and participate in their people's daily struggles and advances.

D. Encourage the return and create the means for the rehabilitation of Eritreans forced to flee their country and land by the vicious aggression and oppression of Ethiopian colonialism.

## 10. Respect the Rights of Foreigners Residing in Eritrea

A. Grant full rights of residence and work to aliens who have openly or covertly supported the Eritrean people's struggle against Ethiopian colonial oppression and for national salvation and are willing to live in harmony with the legal system to be established.

B. Mercilessly punish aliens who, as lackeys and followers of Ethiopian colonialism, imperialism, and Zionism, spy on or become obstacles to the Eritrean people.

## 11. Pursue a Foreign Policy of Peace and Non-Alignment

A. Welcome the assistance of any country or organization which recognizes and supports the just struggle of the Eritrean people without interference in its internal affairs.

B. Establish diplomatic relations with all countries irrespective of political and economic system on the basis of the following five principles: respect for each other's independence, territorial integrity, and national sovereignty; mutual nonaggression; non-interference in internal affairs; equality and mutual benefit; peaceful coexistence.

C. Establish good friendly relations with all neighbors.

D. Expand cultural, economic, and technological ties with all countries of the world compatible with national sovereignty and independence and based on equality. Do not align with any world military bloc or allow the establishment of any foreign military bases on Eritrean soil.

E. Support all just and revolutionary movements, as our struggle is an integral part of the international revolutionary movement in general, and the struggle of African, Asian, and Latin American peoples against colonialism, imperialism, Zionism, and racial discrimination in particular.

**Victory to the Masses!**

# Chronology of Significant Events

1884–85    The Conference of Berlin results in the division of Africa into European spheres of influence.

1884–97    Ethiopian Emperor Menelik's Shoan kingdom expands tenfold to become the Ethiopian empire.

1889       Italy declares Eritrea its colony. Ethiopia recognizes this fact with the signing of the Treaty of Ucciali.

1896       Menelik's forces, replenished with men and supplies from southern conquests, defeat the Italian army at Adwa.

1897       An Anglo-Ethiopian treaty recognizing Menelik's conquest of the Ogaden (Western Somalia) is signed.

1897       Mohammed Abdille Hassan begins armed resistance among the Somali, which continues until his death in 1920.

1916       Emperor Haile Selassie (then Ras Tafari Mekonnen) successfully leads a *coup d'état* against Menelik's chosen successor.

1930       Ras Tafari Mekonnen is crowned emperor of Ethiopia under the throne-name Haile Selassie.

1931       Haile Selassie promulgates a written constitution.

1936       Mussolini's Italian colonial army invades Ethiopia, driving Haile Selassie into exile.

| | |
|---|---|
| 1941 | The Italian army is defeated by British-led forces in Somalia, Ethiopia, and Eritrea. |
| 1943 | The Somali Youth League is established in Mogadishu, renewing the pan-Somali nationalist movement. |
| 1950 | The United Nations General Assembly decides on the future of the former Italian colonies: Libya is to become independent in 1953; Somalia is to be administered under a UN trusteeship system, with Italy the administrator, for ten years, after which it is to become independent; and Eritrea is to be "federated" with Ethiopia. |
| 1952 | The "federation" of Ethiopia and Eritrea comes into effect. |
| 1953 | Libya becomes independent. A U.S.-Ethiopian treaty is signed, giving the United States a base in Asmara, along with other facilities, for twenty-five years. |
| 1955 | A revised constitution is promulgated in Ethiopia. |
| 1956 | The Sudan becomes independent. Broadcasts from Cairo in Tigrinya and Arabic begin to be heard in Eritrea. |
| 1957 | Tigrinya and Arabic are abolished as the official languages of the Eritrean government, in violation of the UN resolution. Student boycotts and demonstrations begin. |
| 1958 | Labor unions in Eritrea stage a general strike. Police fire on demonstrators, killing and wounding several hundred. |
| 1959 | The Eritrean Liberation Movement (ELM) emerges. |
| 1960 | Somalia becomes independent. |
| 1960 | Haile Selassie's bodyguards attempt a coup. |
| 1961 | The Eritrean Liberation Front (ELF) is established. |
| 1962 | Haile Selassie unilaterally abolishes the "federation" of Eritrea and Ethiopia. |
| 1963 | The Organization of African Unity (OAU) is established at a meeting in Addis Ababa. |

1964    A resolution is passed at the second meeting of the OAU in Cairo accepting the colonially established boundaries throughout Africa.

1964    There is an Ethiopian-Somali border clash.

1969    A military coup in Sudan, led by Nemiery, overthrows the civilian government of Saddik el Mahdi.

1969    A military coup in Somalia, led by Siad Barre, overthrows the government of Ibrahim Egal.

1970    The Eritrean People's Liberation Front (EPLF) is formed out of ELF splinter groups.

1972    The Somalian military government issues a charter indicating its socialist program.

1972–73  Drought in the Horn and Sahelian regions of Africa.

1974    Haile Selassie is overthrown by a popular uprising, which is then usurped by the military.

1975    The civil war between the ELF and the EPLF comes to an end. In February, an Ethiopian military offensive brings the war into the highlands.

1975    The Ethiopian military government announces the abolition of the feudal land tenure system, as well as other radical measures.

1976    The Supreme Revolutionary Council of Somalia forms the Somali Revolutionary Socialist Party, whose program is proclaimed in July.

1977    The first congress of the EPLF is held in the liberated zone of Eritrea.

1977    Djibouti becomes independent.

1978    The Soviet-backed Ethiopian armed forces, with Cuban help, reconquer the main cities of the Ogaden and some liberated cities in Eritrea.

1979    A fifth Ethiopian offensive, aimed at capturing Sahel base areas in Eritrea, fails. The EPLF gains the initiative and some lost ground.

1979    The Dergue announces the formation of a commission to establish a party, with Mengistu as chairman.

# Notes

*Introduction*

1. The Sudan is also geographically a part of the region, but is not included in what is commonly referred to as the Horn of Africa. Aspects of Sudanese politics will nevertheless be discussed as they impinge on the politics of the Horn.
2. Rupert Emerson, *Self-Determination Revisited in the Era of Decolonization* (Cambridge, Mass.: Harvard University Press, 1964), pp. 28–32. See also Bereket H. Selassie, "The Evolution of the Principle of Self-Determination," *Horn of Africa Journal* (Winter 1978–1979).
3. The Biafra war of secession is another example of a national crisis rooted in colonial history. One difference is that the struggle in the Ogaden continues. Another is that President Nyerere of Tanzania supported the Biafra cause on the principle of the right of the Ibo nation to self-determination, yet he has failed to support the Somali's right to self-determination in the Ogaden, which is based on the same principle. He also chose to ignore the fact that the Eritrean question is a colonial one. He seems to have chosen not to burn his fingers again. On the other hand, he reversed himself again when he intervened in 1979 in Uganda in the invasion to overthrow Idi Amin. This invasion may have opened the way for a reappraisal of the OAU charter, as the proceedings of the OAU summit in Monrovia indicate.

## Chapter 1.  Ethiopia: Empire-State

1. Men for the most part inherited *rist*, although in a few areas women also had *rist* rights. I observed the Ethiopian legal process as a law teacher and as a "captive official" in the government between 1956 and 1964, when I resigned and was later exiled to Harar.
2. John Markakis and Nega Ayele, *Class and Revolution in Ethiopia* (London: Spokesman Press, 1978), p. 22.
3. The northern region of Ethiopia, inhabited by the Amhara and the Tigray nations, is predominantly Christian. The southern and southeastern regions, by contrast, are predominantly Muslim.
4. For an excellent analysis of the intricacies of the Amhara land tenure system, see Allan Hoben, *Land Among the Amharas of Ethiopia* (Chicago: University of Chicago Press, 1973).
5. Markakis and Nega, *Class and Revolution in Ethiopia*, p. 26.
6. Ibid., pp. 24–25.
7. Ibid., p. 25.

## Chapter 2.  Ethiopia: Empire and Revolution

1. The sector review was a World Bank-inspired educational reform project involving a redistribution of educational opportunities and therefore a financial reallocation that negatively affected the teachers' salaries. This was a major reason for the teachers' revolt on the eve of the revolution. The teachers felt that they were a neglected stratum of the professional class, with no government commitment for the improvement of their position—i.e., no definite schedule for salary increases and promotion. The most politically conscious among them were to exercise a decisive influence in turning the teachers into agents of the revolution, a role they began to play when they attacked the sector review and analyzed its defects. They won the support of parents, who feared that the sector review was designed to deny their children the opportunity of higher education.
2. See John Markakis and Nega Ayele, *Class and Revolution in Ethiopia* (London: Spokesman Press, 1978), p. 82.
3. Ethiopian students in Europe played a significant role in publicizing the disaster. Dimbleby, in his testimony before the Ethiopian

Commission of Enquiry, noted that he first learned of the disaster in this way.

4. Both these "facts" are disputed. Mengistu was brought up and educated, until he joined the Holeta Cadet School, by Dejasmatch (duke) Kebede Tessema, who had been a close servant of Empress Zewditu, Haile Selassie's predecessor, and then became a close confidant and faithful servant of Haile Selassie himself. Mengistu's mother was one of Kebede's housemaids, but it has never been proven either that he is an illegitimate son of Kebede or the son of a slave. Kebede has maintained his contact with Mengistu, and has advised him on strategies to eliminate his rivals. Further, Mengistu has not been proven to be an Oromo, although he has hinted that he is. This belief, along with the fact that Haile Fida was Oromo, gained support for the Dergue from elements of the Oromo nation at a critical stage.

5. According to conversation he had with me immediately after his resignation.

6. Aman's friends, myself included, tried to persuade him to escape, but he told us, "I will not turn my back and run. I am a general, and if they come to arrest me, I will not be led out of my house like a sheep." Some officers in fact wanted to kidnap him for safekeeping, but were too late.

7. Markakis and Ayele, *Class and Revolution in Ethiopia*.

8. Curiously, however, Haile Fida was apparently carefully monitoring Sisay's movements and reporting them to Mengistu. Mengistu and Haile were very close at the time, and were probably suspicious of Sisay's ambition, each for his own reasons.

9. *The New African* (London), November 1979.

## Chapter 3. Eritrea: A Colonial Struggle

1. See P. M. Holt, *The Mahdist State* (Oxford: Clarendon Press, 1970), esp. pp. 45–65.

2. See J. S. Trimingham, *Islam in Ethiopia* (London: Oxford University Press, 1952); G. K. N. Trevaskis, *Eritrea: A Colony in Transition, 1941–1952* (Westport, Conn.: Greenwood Press, 1975); E. Ullendorf, *The Ethiopians* (London: Oxford University Press, 1973).

3. On Menelik's dealings with Italy, see Carlo Rossetti, *Storia Diplomatica dell' Etiopia* (Torino, 1910).

4. Trevaskis, *Eritrea*, p. 33.

5. Article 23 of the treaty; see also paragraph 3 of Annex II.
6. See Resolution 289A (iv).
7. See Articles 1 and 55 of the charter.
8. *Market International Report* (Ethiopia summary), January 1977, quoted in Linda Heiden, "The Eritrean Struggle for Independence," *Monthly Review* (July–August 1978), p. 15.
9. In a written statement he submitted to the Commission of Enquiry established in 1974 to investigate Haile Selassie's government. Documents released under the U.S. Freedom of Information Act prove beyond doubt the role of the United States and its Western allies in the UN "disposal" of Eritrea.
10. "Kagnew" was the name of the battalion that was sent to fight in Korea. It was also the nom de guerre of Ras Mekonnen, Haile Selassie's father.
11. Final Report of the United Nations Commissioner for Eritrea, chapter 2, p. 201. For a detailed discussion of this point, see my paper presented to the Permanent People's Tribunal, Milan, May 27, 1980.
12. The paradox of this relationship in constitutional terms is described by the eminent British professor of constitutional law, Ivor Jennings, in *Approach to Independence* (London: Oxford University Press, 1956). Jennings was one of the three legal experts who drafted the Eritrean constitution.
13. See the preamble to the UN resolution cited above.
14. Wolde-Ab was a master of the Tigrinya language, both in spoken and written form, and his use of proverbs and simple stories appealed to the masses. Others made broadcasts in Arabic to good advantage.
15. Osman Saleh Sabbe, *The Root of the Eritrean Disagreement* (Beirut, 1978), p. 41.
16. Ibid., p. 42.
17. I personally observed new recruits joining by the thousands in the hills of the Hamasien highlands in late 1974 and early 1975.
18. See Appendix 3.
19. See the EPLF communiqué entitled "Condemn Soviet Aggression in Eritrea," New York, December 7, 1978.
20. See the interview with Ramadan Mohamed Nur, secretary-general of the EPLF, and Issayas Afeworki, its deputy-secretary, by Jean-Louis Peninou, *Liberation* (March 1979).
21. For details of this EPLF offensive, and its consequences, see the EPLF press release, January 6, 1980.

## Chapter 4. Oromo and Tigray

1. L. Harry Gould, *Marxist Glossary* (San Francisco: Proletarian Publishers, 1941), p. 68.
2. V. I. Lenin, *Collected Works* (Moscow: Progress Publishers, 1964), vol. 22, p. 146.
3. Ibid., p. 143.
4. Ibid.
5. Ibid., p. 147.
6. This material is well summarized by Herbert S. Lewis in an article in *Journal of African History* 7, no. 1 (1966), pp. 27–46.
7. *Some Records of Ethiopia, 1593–1646; Being Extracts from "The History of High Ethiopia or Abassia" by Manoel de Almeida, together with Bahrey's "History of the Galla,"* edited and translated by C. F. Buckingham and G. W. B. Huntingford (London, 1954), pp. 111–12. See also Lewis, p. 32.
8. The first figures appear in Donald N. Levine, *Greater Ethiopia: The Evolution of a Multi-Ethnic Society* (Chicago: University of Chicago Press, 1974), p. 38; and the second in a press release issued by the Union of Oromo Students in Europe on January 17, 1978, and quoted in P. T. W. Baxter, "Ethiopia's Unacknowledged Problem: The Oromo," *The Royal African Society (African Affairs)* 77, no. 308 (July 1978), p. 255.
9. Quoted in Baxter, "Ethiopia's Unacknowledged Problem," p. 255.
10. Ibid., p. 289.
11. Ibid., p. 259.
12. See OLF, *Bakkalcha Oromo*, OLF's Program (1976), distributed in the United States by the Union of Oromo Students in North America. All subsequent quotes are from this document.
13. The program has a section on international relations that indicates the anti-imperialist stand of the OLF, but its support of the Eritrean struggle falls short of recognizing it as a colonial question. The relevant section reads: "[The OLF] supports the Eritrean peoples' struggles for self-determination that are being waged in the empire-state of Ethiopia."
14. See *Kara Wallabuma* (bulletin of the Union of Oromo Students of Europe) 2, nos. 2–3 (November–December 1977), p. 71.
15. See *Waldaansoo* 2, no. 2 (May 1978), p. 20.
16. The TPLF program speaks of the people of Tigray as those living

within Tigray, whether they speak Tigrinya, Afar, Agaw, Saho, or Kunama, and those living outside Tigray.

17. See *Tigray: A Nation in Struggle* (Khartoum: TPLF Foreign Relations, October 1979).

18. *Tigray* 2, no. 1 (December 1978), p. 2; this is the newsletter of the Tigreans of North America.

19. *Weyyin* 2 (1978), p. 6.

20. Ibid., p. 7. A detailed list of the booty captured from the EPRA is also included.

21. Ibid., p. 7.

22. *Weyyin* 3 (August 1978), pp. 7–8.

23. *Economist* (London), September 1, 1979.

24. See in particular *Weyyin* 2 (1978), pp. 8–27, 46–53. It has also started broadcasting from Radio Liberation in Eritrea.


## Chapter 5. Somalia: Lost Territories

1. See I. M. Lewis, *Peoples of the Horn* (London: International Affairs Institute, 1955).

2. Saadia Touval, *Somali Nationalism* (Cambridge, Mass.: Harvard University Press, 1963), p. 10.

3. Ibid., p. 14.

4. Henri de Monfried, *Ménélik, Tel qu'il fut?* (Paris: Grasset, 1954), pp. 165–67. For an insightful short history of Harar and its neighbors in the nineteenth century, see R. A. Caulk, "Harar Town and Its Neighbors in the Nineteenth Century," *Journal of African History* 18, no. 3 (1977).

5. See I. M. Lewis, *A Modern History of Somalia: From Nation to State* (London, 1965), p. 41.

6. John Drysdale, *The Somali Dispute* (New York: Praeger, 1964).

7. Anthony Eden statement, House of Commons, quoted in ibid., p. 53.

8. House of Commons Debates, June 4, 1946, cols. 1840–41.

9. Report of the Italian Government to the United Nations General Assembly on Somalia, 1959; French version, italics added.

10. This account is based on my personal observations, made on a visit to Gode in 1969.

11. Many of these recruits were later incorporated into the Somali army, in various ranks, and some were to lead the subsequent

struggle in the Ogaden. See Colin Legum and Bill Lee, *Conflict in the Horn of Africa* (London, 1978), p. 33.

12. On this and much of what follows, see Patrick Gilkes, *The Dying Lion* (London: Friedmanns, 1975).

13. Legum and Lee, *Conflict in the Horn of Africa*, p. 33.

14. Author's interview with Siad Barre. Mengistu and Siad did not meet face to face; instead Castro and Podgorny acted as running intermediaries.

15. According to Cuban officials present at the talks. See *Africa News*, March 13, 1978, p. 8.

16. James MacManus, *The Guardian* (London), September 15, 1976.

17. For example, at the OAU meeting in Mauritius in July 1975, the Ethiopian delegation tried to get a resolution calling for independence postponed.

18. *The Guardian* (London), September 16, 1976.

19. See Legum and Lee, *Conflict in the Horn of Africa*.

20. I. M. Lewis, "Pan-Africanism and Pan-Somalism," *Journal of Modern African Studies* 1 (1963), pp. 47–61.

21. Alexander Melamid, *The Geographical Review*, vol. 54 (1964), p. 587.

22. A. A. Castagno, "The Somali-Kenyan Controversy: Implications for the Future," *Journal of Modern African Studies* 2 (1964), pp. 165–88.

23. Ibid., p. 176.

24. See Colin Legum and John Drysdale, eds., *African Contemporary Record, 1968–1969* (London, 1969), p. 202.

25. See, for instance, Samuel De Calo, *Coups and Army Rule in Africa* (New Haven: Yale University Press, 1976).

26. See Basil Davidson, "Somalia in 1975, Some Notes and Impressions," *Issue* (Spring 1975).

27. See, for instance, *Lisane Abyot* (journal of the Ethiopian Students of North America) 3, no. 9 (October–November 1977).

28. Nor are the Ogaden and Eritrean situations peculiar in this respect. The invasion of Kampuchea by Vietnam and of Uganda by Tanzania, whether or not one supports the invaders' motives, illustrate a similar failure of international legal order.

29. D. Ottaway, *The Washington Post*, July 30, 1977.

30. Informed sources, interviewed by the author.

31. Ibid.

32. Hassan Haile, interview in Mogadishu, October 8, 1979.

Chapter 6. The Big Powers

1. See Fred Halliday, "Report from the Horn of Africa: The Myth of the Super-Powers," *TNI Communication* 1, no. 3 (May–June 1978).
2. "The War in the Horn of Africa." Editorial in the London *Times*, January 19, 1978.
3. See James Buxton, "The Russian Gamble in Ethiopia," *Financial Times*, January 19, 1978.
4. Ibid.
5. Castro's hasty judgment of Mengistu will turn out, in retrospect, to be one of the most serious mistakes he has made in recent years.
6. As stated by the Soviet representative to the United Nations in a debate on the future of Eritrea in 1950.
7. See *Weekly Review*, March 20, 1978, p. 16.
8. Ibid.
9. J. G. Liebenow, "The Caucus Race: International Conflict in East Africa and the Horn," *East African Series* 11, no. 1 (July 1977), p. 2.
10. As reported by the EPLF representative at a symposium on Eritrea in London, January 12–14, 1979.
11. See, for example, John Stockwell, *In Search of Enemies: A CIA Story* (New York: W. W. Norton, 1978).
12. See Scott Thompson, "The American-African Nexus in Soviet Strategy." Paper presented at the 1977 Annual Conference of the American Association for the Advancement of Slavic Studies, Washington, D.C.
13. On the two schools of thought, see Chester A. Crocker, "The African Setting: Two Views on the Horn," *Washington Review of Strategic and International Studies* (April 1978). On the "grand design" and "opportunism" theories, see Dimitri Simes in ibid.
14. See Colin Legum, "The African Environment in the USSR and Africa," *Problems of Communism* (January–February 1978), pp. 1–99. Legum cites the works of Soviet Admiral of the Fleet Sergey Gorshkov, who describes the new Soviet requirements for a system of naval and air facilities.
15. Ibid.
16. David E. Albright, "Soviet Policy," *Problems of Communism* (January–February 1978), pp. 20–29.
17. Dimitri K. Simes, "Soviet Intervention in the Horn," *Washington Review* (April 1978).

18. Richard Lowenthal, "Soviet Counter-Imperialism," *Problems of Communism* (November–December 1976), pp. 52–63.
19. Simes, "Soviet Intervention in the Horn."
20. Fred Halliday, "U.S. Policy in the Horn of Africa: *Aboulia* or Proxy Intervention?" *Review of African Political Economy*, no. 10 (September–December 1978).
21. Crocker, "The African Setting."
22. Ibid.
23. Ibid.
24. Halliday, "U.S. Policy in the Horn of Africa," p. 15.
25. Ibid., p. 14.
26. Ibid., p. 17.
27. Arnaud de Borchgrave, "Crossed Wires," *Newsweek*, September 28, 1977.
28. Thompson, "The American-African Nexus in Soviet Strategy," p. 10.
29. See Raul Valdes Vivó, *Ethiopia: The Unknown Revolution* (Havana, 1978), particularly the foreward which quotes Castro's remarks on the Ethiopian revolution. See also the joint communiqué issued following Castro's visit to Ethiopia in September 1978, in *Granma*, October 1, 1978.
30. Ibid., pp. 20, 30.
31. Interview with sources which must remain nameless. See also Nelson P. Valdés, "Cuban Foreign Policy in the Horn of Africa," *Cuban Studies* 10, no. 1 (January 1980), pp. 50–80.
32. Personal conversation with sources close to the Cuban leadership.
33. Valdes Vivó, *Ethiopia: The Unknown Revolution*, p. 31.
34. See Frank T. Fitzgerald, "A Critique of the 'Sovietization of Cuba' Thesis," *Science and Society* 42, no. 1, p. 16.
35. Cited in ibid., p. 16.
36. Ibid., p. 17.
37. Dan Connell, *The Guardian* (London), January 3 and 10, 1978. Later reports put the number of Soviet officers at 600, and one Russian lieutenant-colonel was reported killed in combat in Sahel. See *Le Monde*, May 26, 1979.
38. Halliday, "U.S. Policy in the Horn of Africa," p. 23.
39. It also enabled him to embark on an adventurist one-man diplomatic initiative to settle the Arab-Israeli conflict, arousing Saudi irritation. Sadat did not consult the Saudis before he took off on his visit to Jerusalem and subsequently to Camp David. One significant,

although little reported, result was a reconciliation between the Syrians and the Iraqis, leading to a United Arab Front opposed to Sadat's initiatives. This has aligned the Saudis rather awkwardly with radical Arab governments.

40. Thomas W. Lippman, *The Washington Post*, March 4, 1979.
41. Ibid.
42. Ibid.
43. Richard Burt, *New York Times*, February 27, 1979.

## Chapter 7.  Neighbors and Meddlers

1. Christopher Batsche, "Le Soudan, peut-il devenir le grenier?" *Le Monde Diplomatique*, January 1978.
2. *Africa Magazine* 83 (July 1978), p. 85.
3. Fred Halliday, "Report from the Horn of Africa: The Myth of the Super-Powers," *TNI Communications* 1, no. 3 (May–June 1978).
4. Ibid., p. 28.
5. See Jean Doresse, *Ethiopia* (London, 1959), pp. 115–19, esp. p. 116.
6. In Sudan, a military government, led by Ibrahim Abhoud, had been established in 1958, but it was done under an arrangement made between the then prime minister, Abdallah Khallil (a former army officer), and Abhoud to forestall an impending political crisis caused by dissent among the main parties. Abhoud's government was overthrown by a popular mass uprising in October 1964.
7. Quoted in Colin Legum, "The African Environment in the USSR and Africa," *Problems of Communism* (January–February 1978), pp. 12–13.
8. Ibid.
9. I was told this story by a former member of the Dergue.
10. This and subsequent quotations come from *Sudan Bulletin* 3 (April 1978), issued by the Central Committee of the Communist Party of the Sudan.

# Index